Perfect Harmony

By Scott Gray
Published by Ballantine Books:

HEART SONG: *The Story of Jewel*
ON HER WAY: *The Shania Twain Story*
PERFECT HARMONY: *The Faith Hill & Tim McGraw Story*

Perfect Harmony

The Faith Hill &
Tim McGraw Story

Scott Gray

BALLANTINE BOOKS • NEW YORK

A Ballantine Book
Published by The Ballantine Publishing Group
Copyright © 1999 by Scott Gray

Cover photo © Lisa Rose/Globe Photos

www.randomhouse.com/BB/

Library of Congress Catalog Card Number: 99-90027

ISBN 0-345-43412-9

Manufactured in the United States of America

First Edition: June 1999

10   9   8   7   6   5   4   3   2   1

Contents

Acknowledgments

"My Heroes Have Always Been Cowboys," was how Willie Nelson titled one of his songs. You gotta love that, but I have to admit that my heroes have always been musicians—people like Willie, who "bowl into the fray" and also have the gift for telling us what it means to them.

I was inspired to write about Tim and Faith because they're fine musicians. But there is more to it. Yes, they've come a long way in their lives, touched so many people with their music. But, most inspiring to me, they aren't just cruising through life trying to grab as much as they can carry. Tim and Faith have bagged that elusive animal that LeAnn Rimes sings about: commitment. Here are two folks treating each other right, living for their children, and making great music, too. In short, Tim and Faith are givers who deserve every reward life sends their way.

ACKNOWLEDGMENTS

Special thanks to Cathy Repetti, Mark Rifkin, Betsy Flagler, Nancy Delia, and Caron Harris.

Introduction

> "We both sang into the hairbrush in front of
> the mirror when we were kids."
> —TIM and FAITH

It's the life of a touring musician: Days roll into days on the road, but at night, when you hit the stage and the audience is on your side, time stops right where you want it to, like in the middle of a beautiful dream. If you are the type who feeds off those moments—and why would you be there if you weren't?—then you summon all the gifts God gave you and try to levitate every soul in the house, at least until it's time to get back on the bus.

Sure it takes incredible energy and focus to perform on a spotlit stage in a packed hall, singing your heart out like Faith Hill and Tim McGraw do each evening when they're on tour. But that's nothing compared to what it takes to keep pace with their toddler daughter, Gracie Katherine. "We get off the bus in a new city, we get her little walker out, and she just goes crazy," Faith explained to Gary Chapman on TNN's *Prime Time Country*. "We just love to watch her go and discover a new place each time we're in a different city."

That, in a nutshell, is what makes Faith and Tim unique within the music business— the fact that they're so doggone normal. This is a point Faith stresses in interview after interview, but it isn't false modesty or pop populism, it's just true. Idolized by thousands and admired by millions, their lives are centered around a love for their daughters and each other that is deep and simple. For them it's all about family. "We love kids. We want to have more," Tim asserts. "Part of our whole life plan is to work hard while we can, and then raise babies." For Faith's part, even before she met Tim her intention to have and raise a houseful of children was clear. As far back as 1995 she spoke of the subject in *CountryBeat*, saying, "That is very important to me. And I'm going to make it happen!"

Life on the road means wild times to a lot of performers, but not to Tim and Faith. There's something downright wholesome in their approach, call it a sense of shared purpose, that shines through clear as winter sunlight to anyone who's ever watched Tim playing with Gracie or seen Faith look after Maggie Elizabeth, who is fifteen months Gracie's junior. It's the kind of relationship that seems made in heaven and kissed by angels. No wonder folks in Nashville have begun viewing Tim and Faith as the new Mr. and Mrs. Country Music.

Tim and Faith wave off that kind of talk, flattering though it might be; in fact, they prefer not to be taken as a duo with regard to their respective careers. "We both have our own careers, and we're both very focused on them and how we want them to progress," Tim has explained. That's reasonable, as both were successful on their own merits long before they became Music City's showcase couple.

In terms of commercial success and artistic honors, Tim is in a league with Garth Brooks, Shania Twain, and LeAnn Rimes; in other words, the top names in the business. Since 1994, he has racked up over $125 million worth of sales. He has won Album of the Year from both the Academy of Country Music

(Not a Moment Too Soon) and the Country Music Association *(Everywhere)*. His 1998 hit "Where the Green Grass Grows" became the eighth number one single of his career.

Yet he is perhaps the least aggressively marketed of his upper-echelon peer group. As he put it to Mike McCall in the *Los Angeles Times*, "I don't go out there searching for reasons to be in the press." He's one of those rare stars who truly hasn't let success go to his head. His friend and coproducer, Byron Gallimore, says this on the subject of Tim's rise from rural kid to superstar, "He was down-to-earth then, and he's down-to-earth now." A cliché perhaps, but everyone says it couldn't have happened to a nicer guy. Daryle Singletary ("I Let Her Lie," "Too Much Fun") once told *Country Weekly*, "I worked with Tim two years ago when I first came out. He was the most cordial person. . . . I think he deserves what he's getting because he's doing what comes from the heart."

Faith, too, is a household name, even if she hasn't equaled her husband's overall sales figures. Unusually long waits between albums account for much of the gap. "Wow, it has been three years," she said of the span between her second and third albums. She was derailed by throat surgery between albums one and two; then she all but disappeared from the scene between albums two and three. "It really wasn't something that was planned," she once told Jim Caligiuri. "I took a year and a half off the road to work on [Faith] and to have a family."

But Faith has been ultraconsistent with her attempts, scoring double platinum on all three releases to date. She is the first female country singer to have her initial three albums sell at least two million copies each. *Contemporary Musicians* biographer Pamela Shelton assessed Faith's place in the Young Country movement like this:

The beautiful blonde vocalist has come to embody the future of country music to a new generation of listeners. Bravely addressing social issues like domestic violence, women's rights, and the need for personal independence within her traditional country sound, Hill is esteemed as a role model for her young country music fans, while helping this traditional American musical genre navigate the modern world.

Like her much-honored husband, Faith has taken her share of awards, the culmination of a lifetime dream. "During my classes in school, I'd daydream about being on stage, especially awards show nights." Early in her career she was a CMT Europe Rising Star and the TNN/Music City News Star of Tomorrow. She was voted Best Female Country Artist in a *Performance* magazine readers' poll, as well as being *Billboard*'s Top Female Country Star. She brought home the CMA's Music Video of the Year prize in 1998 for her crossover smash "This Kiss." In a time when women are getting unprecedented recognition in Nashville, Faith is at the forefront. She sang for billions of people across the globe at the 1996 Olympic Games in Atlanta.

So both Tim and Faith were and are stars in their own right, regardless of the links that bond them. Still most folks can't help but connect Faith and Tim, not only as a couple but as artists, in large part because of one special song: the multiaward-winning smash, "It's Your Love." It's one of the most beloved songs in recent country music history, and it figures to be in rotation on programmer playlists for years to come.

* * *

"The song was magical for the two of us when we recorded it. It didn't feel like anyone else was there—we were in our own little world."
—FAITH

"It was like a piece of us, and then for everybody to be able to share it with us was great."
—TIM

And share it they did, first on their 1996 Spontaneous Combustion tour, then at the 1997 Academy of Country Music Awards show, when Faith was glowing with pregnancy and love was in the air. "The whole magic of two people who really love each other and are singing honestly is amazing," commented radio programmer Dene Hallam of Houston's KKBQ in *Country Weekly*. The storybook romance seemed to unfold before the eyes of delighted fans, and "It's Your Love" was its love theme.

The song proved to be a commercial gold mine, the first song in twenty years to rank number one on the *Billboard* Hot Country Singles & Tracks chart for six weeks running. Faith's exquisitely passionate harmonizing on "It's Your Love" helped push Tim's 1997 album *Everywhere* to the top of the charts, and he returned the favor by backing her on "Just to Hear You Say You Love Me," a major hit from 1998's *Faith*.

Yet aside from those celebrated duets and shared billing on recent tours, Faith and Tim have taken different career tracks to attain the success they now enjoy together. And before falling in love, their personal lives wound along separate paths as well. What their stories have in common are small-town roots (they grew up less than two hours' drive from each other in the rural South), Nashville aspirations (both left home for Music City soon after high school), and the highs and lows that come with chasing dreams.

To have a successful marriage requires two very independent individuals—a man and a woman who aren't defined by each other but enriched—both of whom share common goals and values. Tim and Faith fit that bill to a tee. No question they've created something special together: two adorable daughters so far, plus a professional synergy that's nothing less than remarkable.

PART ONE

⌒ ⌒

Tim McGraw

"I play hard."

CHAPTER ONE

Growin' Up

"I grew up loving any kind of good music.
But when it came to singing, it always came
out country."
—TIM

As an eleven-year-old boy growing up in Start, Louisiana (a dot on the map not far from the small city of Monroe), Timmy Smith loved sports. Baseball was one of his passions, and he kept collector cards of his favorite players on display in his room. That's nothing unusual; kids all over America did and still do the same thing. But none of them were destined for the incredible shock that young Tim received one afternoon in 1978. Years later his mom would pinpoint the irony, saying, "The funny thing was that he did have his father's baseball cards on the wall before he knew it was his father."

While digging in his mother's closet for an old photograph of himself riding horses with Horace Smith, the man Tim thought was his father, Tim happened to come across his own birth certificate. Confused and upset by what he read, Tim called his mom at work and implored her to come home right away. She did, realizing that something was seriously wrong but not sure what it could be.

Tim had uncovered her deepest secret, that his biological father was none other than Tug McGraw, one of the ballplayers whose cards Tim had displayed in his room. It was a difficult situation, as young Tim tried to come to grips with the strange twist of fate. His mother had planned to tell him the truth about his birth when he was older, but now the cat was out of the bag. She could only attempt to comfort Tim about the fact that the man he knew as "Dad" wasn't his natural father. Tougher still, she had to try to explain why the man who'd helped bring him into the world had never spent one minute with his own son.

Tim's mother, who was born Elizabeth Ann Dagostino but has always been known as Betty, met Tug McGraw long before he became a famous major leaguer. She was eighteen and he was twenty-two. Betty's parents were divorced, and she was living with her mom and sister in a Jacksonville, Florida, apartment. Tug lived downstairs in the same complex. He was a pitcher for the Suns, a minor-league farm club. His full name was Frank Edwin McGraw, but everyone called him Tug.

Betty and Tug were attracted to each other. Although they never dated formally, living in the same complex gave them chances to flirt and talk, either at the pool or on informal visits to each other's apartment. Betty had broken up with her high school boyfriend, and Tug was cute and athletic. One evening, in the aftermath of some turmoil between her estranged mother and father, Betty went to Tug's apartment and bared her soul. One thing led to another, and they wound up having sex.

Filled with remorse, Betty avoided Tug after that night. Her mother didn't know what had occurred, but, as it happens, she decided to move with her daughters to a small house on the beach. Betty felt relieved about the change, but her heart was still heavy. When the time came for her period to start, it didn't, and her relatively carefree teenage life would never be the same. Betty was a talented dancer in the style of *American Bandstand* and *Hullabaloo*. She'd won numerous dance contests and met teen idols like the Dave Clark Five and the Beach Boys. But those times were soon to be memories; she was going to become a mother.

A couple of months later, in the fall of 1966, Betty's parents reunited and moved the family to Louisiana. It was around this time that Tug McGraw was seeing his first action with the New York Mets. Betty hadn't told him that she was carrying his child, and she had no intention of doing so. Two-thirds into the pregnancy, her mother figured out what had happened and insisted on calling Tug in New York. She laid out the facts for him, and he chose to turn his back.

On a warm day, the first of May 1967, Samuel Timothy McGraw entered the world at a clinic in Delhi, Louisiana. Fate had laid out a hard road for his mother, but she was a caring young woman who honestly loved and wanted her child. Tim always would have that in his life, even when practical circumstances weren't on his side.

"There's a preconceived notion that I grew up this rich kid, the son of a baseball player. It wasn't like that at all. . . . It's not like I've been handed a silver spoon."

—TIM

Betty's mother and father eventually separated for good. Betty followed her mother to Rayville, Louisiana, and took a waitressing job at the local bus stop café. She worked hard to keep her baby fed and clothed, but it wasn't easy; sometimes she couldn't even afford to buy formula. When an older man named Horace Smith courted her and then suggested they get married, she agreed. Betty had heard that Tug was planning to get married soon, too, so any hope of his changing his mind and taking responsibility seemed to be lost. Betty felt that at least Tim would have a provider and father figure in Horace, and she would be able to stay home and raise her son. Betty's sister Regina could move in with the newlyweds and help take care of Tim. It seemed the right thing to do.

But there was a problem: Horace had a temper and was sometimes abusive. In her book *Tim McGraw: A Mother's Story*, Betty recounts an incident in which Horace, drunk, was late getting home and became upset about his dinner being cold.

He kept screaming and knocked me down. I got up and went toward the bedroom. He yelled for me to come back to the kitchen and clean up the mess. Then he came at me. Timmy came out of the bedroom in his walker with his big brown eyes looking scared to death. I yelled for Regina to get him and take him outside. At that moment, Horace hit me in the back of the head and I fell to the floor. I just lay there pretending I was unconscious so he would leave me alone.

It wasn't that chaotic all the time, but things between Betty and Horace were almost never ideal. Betty did become pregnant again, and Tim's little sister Tracey was born in September of 1968. Later the family moved to a small house in the country, and Betty became pregnant again. Tim's second sister, Sandy, came along in April of 1971. Even at a young age Tim was protective of his sisters. Despite the usual sibling spats, they always looked up to their older brother.

Not long after Sandy was born, Regina moved out. Betty's life was no fairy tale—at one point, as she recounts in her book, Horace blackened her eye in a rage. She and Horace and the kids moved no fewer than ten times during the course of the marriage, and money was forever tight. In an interview with Michael A. Capozzoli in *CountryBeat*, Tim looked back on one of the places they called home during his childhood. "[We] lived in an old shack that they had been using for a hay barn. . . . I remember waking up and seeing cows in the window mooing so they could get milked at sunrise." Betty did her best to keep her kids safe and content in difficult circumstances, and Tim says he never felt poor or deprived.

Tim grew like the proverbial weed. A fast learner, he'd started walking and talking before he was ten months old. Horace taught Tim to ride horses, which Tim counts as one of his favorite childhood memories. He also excelled in Little League baseball. Tim was very bright, athletic, and creative as a child. Like his mom, he loved music. She would listen to the radio or the record player and sing with Rita Coolidge, Crystal Gayle, and the Beach Boys.

In effect, Tim's musical education began at the earliest possible age. The focus was on country, at least more so than on the myriad other styles—Cajun, zydeco, blues, jazz, etc.— that reached his open ears. Tim recalls, "When I was just four or five years old, I'd ride with my stepfather as he hauled cotton seed to Ft. Worth or Monroe, or such. We'd listen to Merle Haggard, Charlie Rich, and all those guys . . . on eight-track tapes, riding up and down the road in an eighteen-wheeler."

Tim had a talent for singing, too. His first public experience came at the tender age of three, when he stood up in church to sing "Jesus Loves Me." He later sang "The Battle Hymn of the Republic" at a school recital, and he performed in his fifth-grade production of *The Music Man*. Tim was shy about the fuss people made over his singing, but once he got on stage he was a natural.

As an adult Tim has professed a belief in the influence of genetics on child development. His position makes sense when you consider that Tim seemed to be gifted with a knack for sports, just like his birth father. They obviously look alike, and Tim also notes that he and Tug share several similar mannerisms and thought patterns. "We think different because we grew up in different areas," Tim once told Richard Cromelin in the *Los Angeles Times*, "but we also think alike on some things. . . . It's amazing sometimes how much we're alike." But there's nothing more powerful than parental guidance, and Tim bears a great resemblance to Betty in regard to his spirit and work ethic.

Betty survived incredible adversity in her first twenty-seven years, including surviving a bout with cancer, which awakened her to life's possibilities. The troubles that had kept her down made her stronger in the long term, and she decided to strike out on her own. Tim was nine when his mother filed for divorce. He still didn't know the true identity of his biological father—or even that his dad wasn't Horace Smith. The kids at school knew Tim as Timmy Smith.

That changed the afternoon he stumbled upon his birth certificate. After learning the truth Tim was eager to meet Tug for the first time. He was filled with anticipation over what might happen if his famous father was an active ingredient in his life. Betty arranged for them to get together in Houston, and although father and son got along well in their first face-to-face encounter, Tug still wasn't willing to become involved in Tim's life.

Tug told Tim, in effect, that although he hadn't been much of a father, the two could still be pals. "Ain't much I could think at age twelve," Tim told Steve Dougherty in *People*,

"I had a great childhood. If you have great parents, it doesn't matter if you're wealthy or on welfare."
—TIM

"except, 'Cool.' " Betty and Tim were Tug's guests at a ballgame, but when they parted company, it seemed as if nothing more would come of the experience than a memory.

Life went on as usual for all concerned: Tug was a millionaire baseball star, one of the best relief pitchers of his time. Betty worked two jobs and attended school while raising three children. Tim went back to playing sports and collecting baseball cards and doing homework and helping his mom and all the other things a young boy could find to do in, as he would later describe it, "a cotton community, with a gin, a small school, a flashing yellow light and not much else."

If his first love was baseball, the passion was doubly inflamed by the revelation about his father. Certainly his coaches expected more of him when they learned the truth. Tim stopped playing at around sixteen, but he stuck with the sport by coaching younger children. Baseball was in his blood, and so was Betty's dedication to children. From the way he looked after his sisters to the way he worked with the little kids, Tim was a natural father figure, a born nurturer.

Even as a teenager he was good with the youngsters: patient and caring, able to put them at ease and help them have fun. Years later, as an adult, this was the quality that drew Faith to him. "I saw this incredibly fatherly instinct that he had," she said in *People*. "He had this real love for children. I thought 'That man has got to be the father of my children.' "

Although he went from player to coach in baseball, his athletic ambitions were strong as ever. He turned his concentration to basketball. Aside from being on the skinny side, Tim was tall, tough, and well-coordinated, and he excelled on offense, scoring 26 points per game one season, according to his mother, a feat that earned him a scholarship to Monroe Christian High School. There was a time when Tim entertained thoughts of being a pro basketball player.

Tim was also keen on rodeo. He loved horses and was a fine rider, thanks in large part to the afternoons spent riding with Horace. Tim also couldn't help noticing that the ladies loved bronco and bull riders. His mom wasn't about to sign a waiver that would permit her fifteen-year-old to risk his neck hanging on to the back of a bucking animal, so one time Tim forged Betty's signature and gave it a whirl. After being tossed off and winding up sore all over, he swore he'd never forge her signature again, although that wasn't his last time to rodeo ride.

In addition to singing, Tim tried his hand at various instruments. His mom brought home a set of drums that she purchased from the house band at a restaurant where she worked. This was around fourth or fifth grade, circa 1977 or so, and Tim was enthralled by the huge sound of Rush, Styx, and Journey—"all those great arena rock bands," as he puts it. He loved banging the skins and crashing the cymbals, but the racket forced Betty to steer him away from the drums.

It wasn't until college that Tim devoted himself to the guitar. "It was a big commuter school. In the summer, everybody left town," he remembers. "I got bored, bought a guitar [from a pawn shop] and taught myself to play." He sometimes practiced so much that it drove his frat brothers to hide the instrument, and he still takes great pleasure in practicing by himself or jamming with his friends. "He taught himself to play by ear," his mother recalled in *Country Weekly*. "Tim

> "When you're fourteen or fifteen years old and you think about being a rock star or a country singer, the thing you think about is being out onstage in front of screaming fans, beautiful women and throwing your sweat around."
>
> —TIM

could still drive you crazy. He'd never put that guitar down."

Tim isn't a virtuoso guitarist and hasn't taken the tumble into songwriting, but it's a safe bet he can do it if he sets his mind to it. His favorite guitar is a Gretch that dates back to around 1950. It's extra special because when Tim and Faith were first married and in the process of moving in together, Faith had put the guitar in the basement. She hadn't meant any harm, of course, but the instrument warped from the dampness. It hadn't been in the best of shape to begin with, but Faith still felt awful. To make up for her mistake, she had the guitar restored and then gave it to Tim as a Christmas present.

Monroe High School had a choir, and Tim was a member. Once, for a senior concert, he and a friend did a special duet, complete with tuxedos and sunglasses; they performed "Silhouettes" and got a standing ovation. Tim was never enthusiastic about the theory aspect of music, but he was open to different styles and was a "student" of great songs, whatever the genre. The time he spent in choir proved to be a terrific learning experience,

"As far as writing goes, I'm not anywhere near the discipline that I need to have. It's something that I want to do in the future, something I will continue to work on."

—TIM

"I grew up listening to music. I was fascinated with it. I always wanted to be a singer."
— TIM

in part because it exposed him to music that wasn't on the radio.

As for his listening habits at home and in the car, Tim was like most young Americans growing up in the South in the 1980s. He liked some new and some old, some country and some rock. As a kid he adored Elvis; in fact, Tim almost got to see the King in concert once, but a case of the mumps kept the disappointed fifth grader from attending the show. This was near the end of the road for Elvis, and Tim never got another chance to see his hero. He remembers watching the Grand Ole Opry with Horace, Betty, and his sisters on Saturday mornings, so the influence of rock and pop was balanced by that of country.

As a teenager Tim became fascinated with honky-tonk, the music of celebration and guilt, of living hard and then paying for it the next morning. It is one of country music's most resilient forms in part because it springs from a blending of the rural and the urban, giving it a wide-ranging, lasting appeal. It cuts across the lines of race and class and gender in much the same way that the blues do. One of Tim's favorite artists, and one of honky-tonk's

> "I grew up in rural Louisiana. I think my music reflects that."
> —TIM

great heroes, is Merle Haggard. "I knew three Merle Haggard albums word for word."

Merle Haggard grew up listening to the classics of Jimmie Rodgers, Hank Williams, Lefty Frizzell, and Bob Wills. As a young man he spent time in prison for robbery, but he became one of the two biggest figures (along with Buck Owens) in the Bakersfield music scene of the 1960s. Merle's style was a mix of hard-core honky-tonk (à la early George Jones) and the Chuck Berry–spawned rock and roll of the 1950s. Merle was instrumental in helping to make the electric guitar a country staple.

Merle kept making hit records into the 1980s, when Tim was in his teens, but by that time the singers who'd been directly influenced by Owens, Jones, and Haggard were starting to make their mark. These were the so-called New Traditionalists, performers such as Dwight Yoakam, Randy Travis, and George Strait. The latter two, in particular, were huge influences on Tim's development into a country singer.

In addition to all his interests outside of school, Tim excelled in the classroom, despite

"Thank God for George Strait and country music!"
—TIM

the fact that, as he put it, he "never cracked a book." His grade point average was second-highest among his small senior class, and he gave a speech at the graduation ceremony. Tim had come a long way in his young life, and he was doing just fine, but there was one aspect that just wasn't right: his relationship, or lack thereof, with Tug McGraw. "I felt like I was a man at eighteen years old and I needed to pursue it, face him, ask some questions and try to work things out," Tim has been quoted by Gerry Wood in *MusicWorld*.

Betty had never asked Tug to pay for any aspect of Tim's upbringing, and he had never offered, but the time had come for him to do his part. It took negotiations with a lawyer, but Tug agreed to pay for Tim to attend college and to meet with him one more time. At this second face-to-face between father and son, something took hold and made Tug realize what he was missing by avoiding this intelligent, personable seventeen-year-old who was his own flesh and blood. He promised to spring for Tim's entire education, and later he introduced Tim to his other children, Mark and Carrie, Tim's half brother and half sister.

"Betty told me, 'Tug, it's time for you to get involved in this one way or another.' And so I did."
— TUG McGRAW

Since that meeting, Tim and Tug have gotten to know each other, become friends, and reached an understanding. "Things have worked out well," Tug told David Zimmerman in *USA Today*. "There are a lot of unfortunate stories out there, and we're not one of them. We worked things out." Tim doesn't hold a grudge, which is remarkable in this age of adult children who never forgive their parents' shortcomings.

"We both learned a long time ago that you have to put events in your life into proper perspective," Tim told Logan Neill in the *St. Petersburg Times*. "There were times that what he told me wasn't always what I wanted to hear, but I realized that's just the way things are sometimes." Tim couldn't be blamed if he were still to resent the fact that Tug ignored him for so long, but he laughs it off, saying, "He was twenty-two and immature when it happened. Hell, he's still immature."

After some deliberation Tim decided to enroll at Northeast Louisiana State University, as it was close to home and comparatively inexpensive. Tim reportedly turned down some sports scholarship offers, but his mother has been quoted as saying that he entered NLSU

Tim on Tug

"The only song Tug knows is the National Anthem, and he still thinks Elvis is alive."

"He's a nut and fortunately I didn't inherit any of that—well—you might get conflicting reports, but I'll say I didn't."

Tug on Tim

"He likes to tell everybody I'm his older brother. What's scary is sometimes it works."

"When I was in baseball, I tried to take it to an art form. I see Timmy doing that with his music."

"with a full scholarship for his voice." He was also in a musical group with some of his friends. The Electones, as they were known, did a few concerts, including one at the local fair. In her book Tim's mom recalled, "He had all the girls screaming (even then)." Tim had vague plans to work through law school, and he later switched from pre-law to sports medicine, but more and more he was thinking of music as a possible career. "I knew I had to do something that didn't require much of an education," he would later fess up in *People*.

Betty eventually moved back to Florida, and, in time, Tim decided to leave Louisiana and join his mother and sisters in Jacksonville. He enrolled in junior college, but his mind wasn't on his studies. Tim had the fever—he wanted to be a music star. His guitar playing had improved, and he sat in with friends at a few live shows in area clubs. One of his influences during this period was a local musician, James Pastell, who gave Tim deep inspiration. No doubt Tim was heading toward a crossroad: Should he stick to the usual path of school and work or follow a dream?

While in Jacksonville, Tim was working in

a restaurant where, as fate would have it, Randy Travis and his manager came to eat breakfast one morning. Tim wasn't on the job at that moment, but someone called him and he dashed to the restaurant posthaste. It was one of those once-in-a-blue-moon moments, the kind that people remember for the rest of their lives and that take on an air of fable when the participants are Randy Travis and Tim McGraw.

Randy was huge at the time: In 1986 he'd created one of the best debut albums in Nashville history, *Storms of Life*, and the 1987 follow-up, *Always and Forever*, eventually sold five million copies. Tim was eager for advice, and Randy was gracious. He told the aspiring singer that if he wanted to make it in country music, he ought to move to Nashville. Randy's manager added, ". . . if you sing as good as you look, you'll make it in country music."

Tim knew what he wanted to do, but he wasn't quite ready to make the move. Instead, he went back to Monroe and reenrolled at Northeast Louisiana State on a part-time basis. He stepped up his music endeavors and also spent a lot of time playing intramural sports and partying. As he puts it: "I joined a fraternity and learned how to float kegs, and I thought that was a lot more fun."

Something had to give, and his studies were it. Besides, he felt that his true calling was to be a country music singer, and for that to happen he needed to take the good advice Randy Travis had offered him. Tim phoned his mom and asked for her blessing on his decision to leave college early and head to Nashville. Her response was, in a nutshell, "Go for it!"

Tim consulted Tug about the idea, and the initial response was less enthusiastic than Betty's. Tug argued that Tim should finish school first, but Tim pointed out that Tug had left school to play baseball. Tug went to hear Tim sing, and he had to agree. "I knew that was where his heart was," recalls Tug. Tim's college career lasted three years, 1986 through 1989, and his music career was about to begin. He sold most of his possessions—"all my shotguns . . . my car"—and caught a Greyhound bus heading north.

Upon arriving in Nashville, May 9, 1989, the day Keith Whitley died, Tim slept at the Quality Inn Hall of Fame and spent idle hours in the bar buying drinks for songwriters.

"I have no idea why I thought I could be a country singer, other than I couldn't do anything else. I learn fast. That's probably my biggest asset."

—TIM

Eventually he found a roommate and moved into an apartment. Tim worked various jobs (repairing shopping carts was perhaps the most unusual) and made new friends (including country legend Lefty Frizzell's nephew, Jimmy). It was an exciting if uncertain time. Sure, Tim always could give up and go back to Louisiana if his plans didn't come to fruition. But his dream of making country music a career might be riding on what he could accomplish during his first year in Nashville.

While waiting and working for his big break, Tim ate a lot of Flash's Hound hot dogs and performed at Printers Alley nightclubs (the famed center of Nashville nightlife). Skull's Rainbow Room was one of his regular haunts, thanks to friend Jimmy Snyder who frequently let Tim join him onstage. He led the life of most Music City up-and-comers, putting together a band and making the local rounds. Tim and his bandmates hauled their equipment in a beat-up trailer, and themselves in Tim's van.

Money was tight, so Tim and his band tried to stretch each dollar to the limit. They bought cheap nylon roses at department stores and sold them before their shows. The girls in the crowd would throw the roses onto the stage. After the show Tim and the boys would gather up the fake flowers and resell them at the next gig. It was somewhat reminiscent of stunts Tim pulled as a youngster. For instance, if his mother offered to pay him to dig weeds, he might "farm the job" to a younger boy for less money, thus making a profit for doing no work. Some might call it lazy, but it's also smart.

After struggling for a couple of years, working all the while to refine and develop his sound, Tim finally caught the break he needed. A farmer back in Louisiana, a friend of the family, loaned Tim $3,000 to record a demonstration tape. A then-unknown Joe Diffie, who has since had no less than five number one singles, sang backup on one of the two songs on Tim's demo. That song impressed the folks at Curb Records, and Tim was signed to a contract.

Just like that his career was on the launching pad. "It almost seemed too easy," Tim would explain in hindsight to Van Rose in *Country Song Roundup.* "But I found out later just how tough the music business is. It took me a long time to get a hit record."

"I'm not as lazy as I thought I was."
—TIM

CHAPTER TWO

Nashville Callin'

"Ninety percent of what we do is having the
guts to get up there and do it."
—TIM

Ink on a contract is never the guarantee of
overnight success that some folks imagine it
to be. Certainly it's an indication that you're
going in the right direction, but it's more of
a milepost than an ENTERING STARDOM sign.
Tim's situation didn't change much at first. He
was still doing club dates with his band, still
sweating to make ends meet. One night in
New Mexico they were booked into a club
that could hold 1,500 fans, but fewer than
fifty people turned up. The show went on, but
Tim admits his head was hanging when he
went to pick up his check.

But there was at least one new aspect to his

life: making preparations to record his first album. The process of selecting songs for his debut was a learning experience for Tim, and he showed flashes of the hit-picking instinct that can be so crucial for an artist who doesn't write his own songs. Unlike most of the rock-and-roll industry, the Nashville method tends toward a hierarchical division of labor between songwriters, instrumentalists, singers, and producers—there's even a dichotomy between the studio cats who play on albums and the road warriors who play in concert. (For example, you'll hear the drumming of Music City mainstay Lonnie Wilson on most of Tim's albums, but Billy Mason is Tim's live drummer.)

In such a system the choosing of songs is a big part of the artist's creative input. Tim might not write the songs or play the guitar on his albums, but he does help sift through the hundreds of options in search of the elusive "right" song. What's more, he has also become an integral part of the production effort on his albums, and he is also working toward taking on the role of a songwriter.

For his first album, though, Tim's part in the overall process consisted primarily of input on song selection and, of course, singing.

He also came up with the simple, sincere liner notes. Tim expresses thanks for the support of numerous people, but at the end of the credits is an unexplained message: "FOR BURNOUt" FOR BELIEVING. The cryptic dedication is an apparent reference to Mike Reeves, who is the husband of an old friend of Tim's mom. Tim met Mike in Florida, and Mike encouraged Tim to pursue the dream of going to Nashville and becoming a professional singer.

The first song on *Tim McGraw* to be put out as a single was "Welcome to the Club." It's a honky-tonk hurtin' song in which the singer commiserates with a fellow Lonely Hearts Club member. It features a nice blend of poignant steel guitar, plaintive fiddles, and vocal twang, but the production is somewhat pedestrian. The song didn't prove memorable enough to make more than a brief appearance on the *Billboard* charts, and it never cracked the top thirty.

What the song did do was put Tim's name into the minds of at least a few reporters, radio programmers, and concert promoters. The mild success of "Welcome to the Club" led to Tim's chalking up his first shot as a warm-up act for someone famous—Gene Watson. One of the most respected of traditional honky-tonk vocalists, Gene put at least eighteen songs in the *Billboard* top ten between 1975 and 1990. Tim opened for Gene at the Jacksonville State Fair, in the same arena where Betty used to dance as a teenager.

The second single from *Tim McGraw* was a hard-driving, blues-based number called "Memory Lane." The song was cowritten by Joe Diffie, whom Tim once called "the greatest singer in music." (The song's other writing credit goes to Lonnie Wilson, the drummer who has played on all of Tim's albums except for *Tim McGraw*.) "Memory Lane" has a more compelling feel and arrangement than "Welcome to the Club," but it still fell short of expectations on the charts. The album yielded one other single—"Two Steppin' Mind"—a straight-no-chaser honky-tonk dance song. It fulfills its purpose as a boot-scooter but doesn't have a sharp-enough hook to stick with the listener after the music ends.

The Nashville scene is dog-eat-dog and packed with talented hopefuls, all scrambling for chart position and radio airtime. In the same year *Tim McGraw* debuted, country music fans were likewise introduced to Toby Keith, Doug Supernaw, Clay Walker, and

Tracy Byrd, each one of whom managed to generate a number one hit during the course of 1993. It was a hot year for new men in Music City, and Tim failed to register as more than a small blip on the radar screens of most listeners.

To some degree his experience mirrored that of yet another future star whose first album came out in 1993: Shania Twain. Her self-titled debut suffered from run-of-the-mill production and mediocre songs, and, as with *Tim McGraw*, the initial release of *Shania Twain* received little fanfare and resulted in no major hits. Of course, the other trait Tim and Shania have in common is that neither let a slow start turn into defeat. At the end of 1995—two years after few folks would have bet that Tim and Shania were on track for stardom—a Gannett News wire story about music videos noted: "There is enormous investment by the labels to land the next Tim McGraw or Shania Twain."

A huge factor in the eventual "arrival" of both Tim McGraw and Shania Twain was their willingness to court young fans, those teenage and younger who grew up on cola commercials and rock videos and who make up a big percentage of total music sales. Tim and his managers even went so far as to rig up closed-circuit TVs outside of clubs so that underage kids could see the show for five dollars.

At least one source did call Tim's rise to stardom before the fact. Prior to the release of his second album, Tim was pegged by *Country Music* magazine as one of the new artists "most likely to succeed." Then early in 1994, Tim's second album was released. In March of 1994, *Not a Moment Too Soon* made its *Billboard* chart debut. By early April it was number one among country albums, and a month after that it supplanted Pink Floyd's *The Division Bell* at the top of *Billboard*'s album chart for all genres. Tim had come a long way from his first paid shows, in places like the Pig BBQ in Jacksonville and the Cock of the Walk in Louisiana, gigs where he stood in front of some tough crowds and sang "whatever got me out without being hurt."

Not a Moment Too Soon had exploded into the stratosphere, making Tim McGraw an "overnight" sensation. The match that lit the fuse—for both better and worse—was "Indian Outlaw." Tim and his live band, the Dancehall

"Tim McGraw's guitar player was a friend of mine, and Tim was just breaking at the time. The first time we talked it was sort of like, 'Tim who?' You know how things go here in Nashville; they were saying Tim was going to be 'the next Garth.' "

—BILLY MASON

Doctors, had been doing the song in concert, and it always went over well. There was never a question in Tim's mind that it would make a terrific single, and the charts bore out his belief. "Indian Outlaw" peaked at number eight on the *Billboard* country chart and also broke into the top twenty for all genres.

The single was a big hit—over 650,000 copies were sold—but some American Indians considered the lyrics offensive. At the Ham Jam concert in Augusta, Georgia, in June of 1994, attempts were made to convince the local arts council to prevent Tim from singing the song. The council declined, and although there was a small protest outside the arena grounds, the concert went off as planned. A number of radio stations—in Arizona, Minnesota, Nevada, Iowa, Oklahoma, and other states—crossed the song off their playlists in response to the controversy. Buzi Two Lance of South Dakota station KILI was quoted in *Entertainment Weekly* as saying the song is "degrading and racist." There were even protests outside some of Tim's concerts.

Tim was surprised and saddened by the negative response. "*Entertainment Tonight* did a story on it," Tim told Bill Hobbs in *New*

Country. "They just killed me." While in Tulsa for a concert, he met with an advocate who explained to him what, in American Indian culture, is the sacred nature of items, such as the peace pipe, that are mentioned in the song. Tim sent a letter to one of his more vocal critics, stating that he is proud of his grandmother's Cherokee heritage and that he does not use artifacts, costumes, or props while performing the song.

Tim tried to shed a different light on the negative response, stating, "If my record, in a backwards way, can be a springboard for Native American issues to be heard, then I'm glad." He asserted that a number of his fans are American Indian and that those fans have "proudly adopted" the song. ("The kids here like to dance to it," one Cherokee vice chief was quoted in *People*. "If I wasn't old and crippled, I'd dance to it, too.") The insertion of the bridge from the Raiders' hit "Indian Reservation (the Lament of the Cherokee Indian Reservation)" was, in Tim's view, a tribute. It was clear that Tim regretted the hurt feelings, but he had no intention of dropping "Indian Outlaw" from his repertoire.

* * *

"I'm a redneck and I admit it, but when Joe Diffie sings about a dumb redneck climbing up on a water tower and painting 'Billy Bob Loves Charlene,' it doesn't offend me."
—TIM

One of Tim's managers, Tony Harley, expressed that the song's message, outside of its literal subject, is that "people are people . . . and kids will be kids." Tommy Barnes, one of the cowriters, commented, "I know there are some people who might find it offensive. The intent was never to make anyone feel uncomfortable." Barnes, who has said that he is part Cherokee, continued, "Let [those who are offended] be heard. But let me be heard, too."

What about the song that touched off the firestorm? "Indian Outlaw" has been described as a "novelty" song, a somewhat dismissive term that suggests the song isn't to be taken too seriously. The arrangement includes some stereotypical American Indian–style riffs and rhythms, and the lyrics are a hodgepodge of references to wigwams, tepees, tom-toms, and peace pipes. Clichés are part and parcel of most pop songs, and this one is no exception. There's little doubt that it presents a caricature of American Indian legends, based more on John Wayne movies than on real life.

But perhaps that's the point: "Indian Outlaw" describes a mythic figure, half icon and half cartoon. It's roughly akin to the "The Legend of Davy Crockett" in that respect.

Calls for cultural or historical accuracy seem like a bit of a stretch. It's just a pop song, for goodness sake. Brouhahas such as the one that sprung up over "Indian Outlaw" are often due in part to the media's thirst for controversy and the need of politicians to work a soapbox.

Other than providing an easy angle for writers and a cause célèbre for activists, the furor had little effect. Tim's star was on the rise; nothing could hinder it, and there was sparse need for extra publicity. The songs spoke for themselves: While "Indian Outlaw" had sparked a dance craze and put Tim in the center of the limelight, it was the second single from *Not a Moment Too Soon*, the sentimental "Don't Take the Girl," that established him as a heavyweight contender. Tim assessed it like this: "It had a lot to say, and said it simply enough. I mean, it's not real philosophical, but it's something everyone can understand."

"Don't Take the Girl" is a tender ballad that chronicles one man's journey from child to adult, shown through his changing perceptions of the woman he disdains as a youngster but cherishes as a grown-up. "After 'Indian Outlaw,' I wasn't taken as seriously as I wanted to be," Tim later told James Hunter in *Entertainment Weekly*. "The reaction challenged me to prove that I was serious about being an artist." Some insiders have said that Tim's performance of "Don't Take the Girl" at the 1994 Country Radio Seminar was a turning point in his bid for new respect. He left the audience of radio pros, who are notorious for their rowdiness, in stunned silence. The song went on to become Tim's first number one single. Tim became the first country artist in a decade to put out two gold singles within three months of each other.

The next single released was a genuine hip-shakin' honky-tonker, "Down on the Farm." A brick-solid 4/4 backbeat, over-the-top fiddle and steel guitar, and straight-up country lyrics made this a staple anthem on Young Country radio stations across America. "Down on the Farm" kept Tim on the fast track and cleared the lane for his second number one single, "Not a Moment Too Soon."

Tim's mom wasn't alone in her reaction to the song. Fans responded to the inspirational message, which Tim's warm vocals brought to life, making it his biggest hit to that point. Debuting in November of 1994, "Not a Mo-

> "I think that song will be special to me for a long time. The words, taken spiritually, fit my life. God's always been there for me, or maybe I should say with me, and helps me 'Not a Moment Too Soon.'"
> —BETTY "McMOM" TRIMBLE

ment Too Soon" spent nineteen weeks in the *Billboard* top forty and reached number one in early 1995. *American Songwriter* magazine reported that cowriters Wayne Perry and Joe Barnhill would make $150,000 in airplay royalties, plus an equivalent amount in "mechanical" royalties for sales of the album. The B side, "Refried Dreams," also received significant airplay, climbing to number five on the country charts.

In May, Tim made his first working trip to Europe, spending a few days doing interviews and promotions in England and Germany. He didn't perform while overseas, but he did get the chance to see a Hal Ketchum gig at one of London's underground clubs. Hal is a fellow Curb Records artist who has the rare distinction of being a singer-songwriter-drummer, a sort of Nashville version of pop star Phil Collins. In the audience was Jimmy Page, ex–Led Zeppelin guitarist and one of Tim's heroes. "I got to meet him afterward, which was really cool," Tim told Bob Paxman in *Country Song Roundup*. That scene lends insight into Tim's musical leanings: Ketchum, who often falls on the pop-folk side of the country fence; and Page, a rock god who worships country blues.

Not a Moment Too Soon was a massive commercial breakthrough for Tim. It was the biggest-selling country album of 1994, and one of the top five for all genres. It eventually sold over five million copies. Some critics didn't hear what the fans heard, which shouldn't be a surprise. A reviewer for *Entertainment Weekly* wrote this lukewarm assessment: "Formula turbo-tonk, maudlin ballads, and a tenor nearly indistinguishable from every other on radio."

Nashville critics have three basic insults at their disposal. The most popular and obvious is "pop," as found in the *Country Music* review of *Faith* in which the word was used eight times in less than three columns of writing, with the critic wielding it as a past-generation politician might have invoked the epithet "Communist." The other two standard-issue put-downs are gender specific. The one for women adds up to variations on "tramp," and tends to come in the form of references to Shania Twain. The one for men amounts to "generic"—for example the "tenor nearly indistinguishable from every other on radio" comment cited above—with "hat act" being the buzz phrase.

That particular term arose in the wake of

George Strait, who touched off a wave of young male singers who sought to emulate their hero. Most struggled to distinguish themselves, and, just as strangers on the street all look more or less the same until you get to know them, the bulk of the post–George Strait generation was seen as a mediocre collection of hat-wearing crooners, pale imitations of The Man. Of course, critics burned Tim with that brand, too, but his talent and hard work facilitated a break from the "hat act" herd.

Tim is one of the most unassuming and humble people around. He once noted, "I like hearing good reviews, but bad reviews don't surprise me. Sometimes you feel like you're fooling half the people who like you." But more often than not it's the critics who are fools, so quick to plug music into labeled sockets that yield more heat than light. Tim is aware that, although country music fans are some of the most loyal around, he still needs to extend the boundaries and keep his music fresh. As he put it, he didn't want to be "three albums down the road and everybody's heard all I can do." He's committed to continuing to develop as an artist without giving up what got him where he is now. "I don't think I sound like anybody else," Tim asserts, "and that allows me to do a lot of different types of songs. That's exactly what I want to do. I don't want anybody to get bored with me."

While he might have come up short on critical accolades when *Not a Moment Too Soon* was first released, Tim more than made up for it in industry honors at the end of 1994. First he collected an American Jukebox Award for radio airplay frequency. *Not a Moment Too Soon* was selected Best Dance Album at the Country Dance Music Awards. The Academy of Country Music voted him Top New Male Vocalist and chose *Not a Moment Too Soon* as the Album of the Year, which Tim considers the biggest accomplishment of his career to that point.

During his acceptance speech Tim told the audience, "The most memorable thing I did in 1993 was get locked out of my hotel room in nothing but my underwear. What a way to make your public debut. This year's showing is more to my liking." Following the release of his debut album, Tim had attended his first ACM Awards festivities, although he wasn't a nominee. As he puts it, "In 1993, no one knew me from Adam." It happens that while putting a dinner tray in the hallway outside his hotel room, Tim got locked out in nothing but his briefs. He tried hiding behind a vending machine, but soon had to give in and knock on a random door for help. The person who answered was Dan Seals (of England Dan and John Ford Coley fame), who didn't recognize Tim but did let him in to call the front desk.

Despite being in the running for two Country Music Association Awards—Single of the Year (for "Don't Take the Girl") and Horizon Award—Tim was shut out at the CMAs. To come so close but still not reach the final goal wasn't devastating to Tim, it was inspiring. He explained, "It consumes your life. Every time you see George Strait win an award, that's you winning that award, that's you giving that speech." Just like a boy pitching baseballs in the backyard and pretending he's Tug McGraw, Tim has visualized making the most of his career opportunities in Nashville.

"We thought we were onto something—that we had a good album with a good variety of songs. But I don't think we had any idea of what we actually had," Tim said in reference to the unexpected level of success of *Not a Moment Too Soon*. He believes that if you are in it for the long haul, you have to focus on the good things that will happen in the future.

Tim wasn't shut out often at the award ceremonies. He brought home an American Music Award for Best New Country Artist, a Blockbuster Entertainment Award for Favorite CD, and a *Billboard* Music Award for Best New Artist. During his AMA acceptance speech, Tim thanked his mother "for being a dreamer" and for teaching him to be the same.

There was no question that Tim McGraw had arrived and was destined to be a mainstay on the Nashville scene. He had the sales and the awards to back it up, but, more to the point, he was coming into his own. He could write his own ticket, call his own shots. From here on in, whatever limits existed would be self-imposed. Tim explains, "You always have this picture of what you want to become and what you want to do. . . . When you achieve a certain level of success, there's just a different quality and a different level you get to do it at . . . the freedom to do it the way you want to do it."

CHAPTER THREE

Stormin' the Gates

> "Tim never goes back on his word. He is such
> a good man."
> —JO DEE MESSINA

Despite being a tad shy by nature—"I can hide under my hat," he quips when telling how he overcomes onstage jitters—Tim has a reputation for putting on unforgettable live shows. He'll work the crowd into a froth with turbo-tonkers like "Indian Outlaw," and leave 'em in a puddle with a heart-wrenching ballad such as "Don't Take the Girl." He likes to tease and kid with the fans, so it's fitting that his encore of choice is the Steve Miller classic "The Joker." (Tim's version of the song appears on the *South Park* soundtrack album.) As reviewer Michael Kuelker once wrote in the *St. Louis Post-Dispatch*, "Tim

McGraw's star appeal is such that he can inspire more audience fervor with way less grandstanding . . . he rang the audience's chimes throughout the set."

No stranger to the road, Tim once noted, "I can't sleep anywhere but on the [tour] bus. They park it by my house and let me sleep in it all the time so I can get a good night's rest." He recalls that sleeping was easy in his stepdad's tractor-trailer truck, and claims that sleeping on the bus seems natural. He ought to be used to it, as his tour schedule has at times called for 265 concerts in a year. Tim has headlined shows with Little Texas, Blackhawk, Martina McBride, Mindy McCready, and others. He has toured as an opener for modern country giants Dwight Yoakam and Wynnona, the great George Strait (whom Tim honored with the song "Give It to Me Strait," from *Not a Moment Too Soon*) and hot country bands like Sawyer Brown and Diamond Rio.

Tim has a pretty kickin' band himself, the Dancehall Doctors, one of the tightest backing groups in the business. "And what it all boils down to is knowing my job, which is to make Tim McGraw sound as good as I

> "When a concert starts, I can feel electricity in the air, like everybody is with us. I wind up playing above my head."
>
> —TIM

possibly can," is how drummer Billy Mason put it in *Modern Drummer* magazine. The Dancehall Doctors love what they do—and it shows. Tim's concerts tend to be choreographed to a degree, so that all the musicians can nail their cues, but the Dancehall Doctors still manage to be energetic and fun.

It isn't rare for Tim to be mentioned in the same breath as Garth Brooks, whether Tim is doing the talking or not. James Hunter once wrote in *New Country* magazine, "But only one artist has ever seized the scope of Brooks's artistic vision, really: Tim McGraw, whose music sounds little like Brooks's, but who clearly grasped his fundamental message that a revved-up young singer and songwriter might sound less like '50s honky-tonk and more like '70s rock. And still make music that could only be called genuine Nashville country."

Much was made of the fact that *Not a Moment Too Soon* beat out Garth's *The Hits* as the top-selling country album of 1994. The two albums also did battle at the ACM Awards, again with Tim coming out on top. In concert Tim has a few Garth moves under his black hat, such as running down the aisles

"Garth said it best. When you go to a concert, you want to see a show, not hear a CD."

—Tim

(surrounded by security guards, of course) to the stage for the start of his concerts. Garth and Tim have another trait in common: a drive to be their best. "I want to be as big as I can be, if that's in the cards for me," Tim told *What's On* magazine.

That's not to suggest that a rivalry exists between the two singers, but there is common ground. *No Fences*, Garth's breakthrough 1990 album, has been called the cannon shot that touched off the New Country revolution, and there can be little argument that Tim owes Garth a tip of the hat. Also important was the contribution of Clint Black, who overshadowed Garth to an extent when the two debuted in 1989, and whose music and image are said to have been motivating factors in Tim's initial decision to give Nashville a whirl.

The past ten years have seen immense growth and upheaval in Nashville, a big part of which has been the result of an influx of artists who understand the impact of visuals. Style has long been a part of the Nashville equation, but Country Music Television and the like gave birth to a "total package" aesthetic. Watch a block of music videos or an award show and you'll see wall-to-wall hunks and babes.

Television had an undeniable influence on Tim and the other future musicians of his generation. He watched dynamic new stars—Garth, Clint, Dwight, etc.—and pictured himself not only sounding like them but also looking and acting like them. And there is no doubt that Tim was cut from the right cloth when it comes to photogenic looks. At a strapping six feet tall and 165 pounds, he looks a little bit dangerous with his black cowboy hat and neatly trimmed goatee. But his boyish face, easy smile, and friendly eyes reflect a heart of gold, as his legion of fans will testify. Tim is one of the rare breed who comes across as attractive to gals and yet not threatening to guys. And his look translates well onto film. In 1994 he won Male Video Artist of the Year from Country Music Television.

One of the admirable aspects of many members of Tim's generation is that they spent their formative teen years listening to classic rock *and* new wave *and* country, or watching CMT and MTV. As a result their tastes are wide open. "I love all kinds of music

"When I sing it, it's going to be country. But the diversity of the audience allows me a lot more freedom to put more of my influences, like the Eagles, in there."
—TIM

and I love a lot of the other artists that are out there," Tim has often said, and the fact is exemplified in what he lists as his two favorite albums:

Keith Whitley's *Don't Close Your Eyes*

Tim named one of his dogs Whitley in tribute to the late singer-songwriter-guitarist. You might get some debate about whether this is Keith's best album, since the follow-up, *I Wonder Do You Think of Me*, which was released after his death, is also an amazing piece of work, but Tim lists *Don't Close Your Eyes* as his personal favorite. It features the Lefty Frizzell classic "I Never Go Around Mirrors," in addition to the number one hits "Don't Close Your Eyes," "When You Say Nothing at All," and "I'm No Stranger to the Rain," which was the CMA Single of the Year for 1989.

When he was a teenager Keith met his musical soul mate, Ricky Scaggs. For the next ten years or so, the two performed some of the best bluegrass in the land while working with Ralph Stanley's Clinch Mountain Boys. Keith moved to Nashville in 1984, released a couple of good but not great albums, married singer Lori Morgan, and fathered a child. He struck gold with *Don't Close Your Eyes* in 1988, then recorded the seminal *I Wonder Do You Think of Me*. Keith Whitley died of alcohol poisoning on May 9, 1989.

The Little River Band's *Greatest Hits*

Formed in Melbourne, Australia, in 1975, the Little River Band scored major hits with songs such as "Cool Change," "Lady," "Lonesome Loser," "Help Is on the Way," "The Night Owls," and "Reminiscing." (The latter's chorus hook, by the way, is the spit and image of the Antonio Carlos Jobim tune "Wave.") Through the late 1970s and into the '80s, this was one of the most successful FM-radio soft-pop bands in the world. The group underwent several lineup changes during its twenty-plus years, with vocalist Glenn Shorrock fronting all the incarnations.

The Little River Band's sound is similar to the cool pop of the Eagles with less of the country edge. As a matter of fact, ex-Eagles guitarist Glenn Frey joined the LRB onstage at their 1988 reunion concert in Sydney to play renditions of the Eagles' "Desperado," "Lyin' Eyes," and "Take It Easy." The Eagles were one of the biggest influences on Tim's music, and the Little River Band also reflects his taste for this style of music.

Tracing influences can be troublesome these days, as popular music is in a constant state of fusion and flux. Elements that no one thought could coexist have now converged. For instance, Uncle Tupelo's roots reach back to traditional country and punk rock (Roy Acuff meets Iggy Pop). Bela Fleck mixes progressive jazz with bluegrass (Stephan Grappelli meets Bill Monroe). In such a wide-open atmosphere, you'll find unexpected connections between all sorts of musicians and styles.

In the case of Garth, Tim, Shania, Faith, et al.—the mixture is a crowd-pleasing blend of honky-tonk and arena rock (George Jones and Tammy Wynette meet Aerosmith). This rather fun-centric composite hasn't made these artists into critics' darlings, that's for dang sure, but the fans love it, and that's what's important. Tim explained to James Hunter in *Entertainment Weekly*: "The vibe is feel-good. I think Sawyer Brown and Hootie

"The way I sound is the way I am. We lived in a converted hay barn for a year, so I am about as country as you can get. No matter what I sing, it's gonna come out country."

—TIM

"With pop music there's a real void right now. . . . There's no Journey. There's no Rush. There's no Eagles or Pat Benatar. . . . But you're finding more of it in a country format. So I think that audience is coming to us. . . . So I do think that some of us are kinda rockin' country."
—JO DEE MESSINA

[& the Blowfish] have the same attitude. They're happy."

Tim being at his best in a live setting, it was fitting that his next album be debuted live. On the eve of its release to the public, *All I Want* was introduced by Tim himself, live from the studio and broadcast via radio to fans on six continents. Curb had received advance orders for over two million copies of the follow-up to 1994's top album. The runaway success of *Not a Moment Too Soon* positioned *All I Want* as the most anticipated Nashville release of 1995.

Two clichés of the music world are that the follow-up to a breakthrough album is the most difficult of all, and that third albums tend to indicate whether an artist has what it takes for the long haul. Assuming there's a grain of truth to those axioms, *All I Want* was a crux in Tim's career. Would he be able to equal or surpass *Not a Moment Too Soon*—if not commercially then artistically—and was he running out of steam or hitting his stride?

As it turned out, this was the first album for which Tim was given widespread critical acclaim. The same *Entertainment Weekly* reviewer who had given a tepid assessment of *Not a Moment Too Soon* wrote glowingly of

Tim's work on *All I Want*: "His superlative song choice, emotional embodiment of a lyric, and persona—the loser with a heart of gold—make him this year's most deserving underdog." Another critic proclaimed *All I Want* to be Tim's best record, and wrote that Tim "has grown musically and developed into a thoroughly entertaining vocalist." None of this meant that Tim was about to become a critical favorite. *Country Music*, a magazine whose reviewers are engaged in a constant bid to out–old school each other, used phrases such as "emotionally undemanding" and "journeyman singing."

The fans, needless to mention, stamped *All I Want* with their seal of approval, snapping up two million copies during the course of 1995. The album didn't duplicate *Not a Moment Too Soon*'s achievement of being the year's biggest release—Shania Twain saw to that with *The Woman in Me*. But *All I Want* did yield 1995's hottest single, the turbo-tonk classic called "I Like It, I Love It."

A supercharged, good-times love song with a big grin and a whole lotta boogie, "I Like It, I Love It" spent a full five weeks on top of the *Billboard* country chart. That was the longest such stretch for a song since Billy Ray Cyrus's

"Achy Breaky Heart" held on to the number one spot for five weeks in 1992. The protagonist of "I Like It, I Love It" is a dedicated bachelor who has become a devoted boyfriend, thanks to the love of a good woman. The tune is ultra-upbeat, with thunderous drums and a scorching guitar solo. Tim delivers the vocals with his trademark good-natured twang and succeeds in making "I Like It, I Love It" one of the definitive country party tunes of the decade. "I Like It, I Love It" was on the soundtrack of *Something to Talk About*, a feature film starring Dennis Quaid and Julia Roberts. The song has also been the focal point in a series of Bud Lite radio jingles, with Tim doing the voice-overs.

If the leadoff single from *All I Want* was in the lighthearted vein of "Indian Outlaw," the feel of the follow-up was reminiscent of "Don't Take the Girl." Tim has a knack for pouring his heart into a ballad and evoking all the emotions behind a sad story. That's the case with "Can't Be Really Gone," a sobering cry-in-your-beer of a tune that peaked at number two on *Billboard*. The third release from *All I Want* packs a musical and lyrical punch as an anthem for the middle class. "All I Want Is a Life" tells it like it is for all the folks who work their tails off for a piece of pie that never gets served. It was perhaps the most praised song that Tim had ever recorded.

The album's fourth single, "She Never Lets It Go to Her Heart," hit number one in the summer of 1996.

Tim also does a fine job on the songs on this album that weren't put out as singles. "The Great Divide," "Don't Mention Memphis," and "When She Wakes Up (and Finds Me Gone)," are all sincere and moving ballads of broken love. Tim's interpretive range is such that he can infuse a tragic tale with as much pure anguish as he packs unadulterated joy into a party anthem. Terrific up-tempo numbers on *All I Want* include "Maybe We Should Just Sleep on It," "Renegade," and "That's Just Me." Each is among the most popular of Tim's in-concert rave ups.

Not about to let up on the throttle of his revved-up career, Tim spent the bulk of his time on the concert circuit in support of *All I Want*. During Tim's tour with Black-hawk, a guest performer appeared at nine shows, a little-known singer named Jo Dee Messina. She had signed with Curb Records

> "Doesn't everybody think they're Elvis when they're by themselves?"
> —TIM

in 1994, and the label was giving her exposure before the release of her debut album. It isn't uncommon for a record company to place one of its new acts on bills with one of its established stars, but in this instance there was much more to the story.

In the late '80s Jo Dee had pondered the idea of going to law school, then changed her mind and headed off to Nashville in hopes of snatching the brass ring. Sound familiar? Upon her arrival in Music City she met an unknown singer whose circumstances were just about identical to hers: Tim McGraw. The two aspiring artists agreed that if either ever hit the big time, the other would receive a helping hand.

In a strange twist, it once looked as if Jo Dee might be lending Tim a hand. She signed a contract with RCA before Tim was discovered by Curb, and she recalls, "Tim had said, 'When you make it big, don't forget me.' The funny thing is he made it big and didn't forget me." Jo Dee's dealings with RCA didn't result in the release of an album, and she wound up signing with Curb, and by late 1995 she was at work in the recording studio. Tim co-produced Jo Dee's album with Byron Galli-more, who is also Tim's coproducer (with

James Stroud), and the first single, "Heads Carolina, Tails California," shot to number two on the *Billboard* country chart.

Tim has good reason to be proud of his association with Jo Dee. One of his ambitions has been to excel in other aspects of the music business in addition to singing. Tim feels great respect for songwriters, whom he calls "the true artists in this business." But in a town full of fine singer-songwriters, he's earned a reputation as an excellent singer-producer, nurturing a growing publishing company—Breakfast Table Management—on Music Row. Tim's work on Jo Dee's self-titled debut led to him coproducing Jo Dee's follow-up album. He was also in the engineering booth during production of the debut release from a new bluegrass band called the Clark Family Experience, as well as his own 1997 effort, *Everywhere*. "I'm always trying to raise my career higher," he has asserted. "I want to get it as big as I possibly can get it and do it as good as I possibly can do it. But then again, I'm doing better than I ever dreamed I would be doing."

Tim needed to be on hand for each step of Jo Dee's album, so when he was in Nashville to

"He's the real deal: a tremendous vocalist and entertainer and a fine producer."
—DENNIS HANNON, Curb Records

work on his new album, they decided to do them back to back. His production efforts on Jo Dee's albums have won accolades, and he's helped boost his old friend's career. Her superb 1998 album *I'm Alright* (featuring the number one hit "Bye, Bye") has a deep, wide-open sound that will blow the doors off your truck. Jo Dee and Tim are birds of a feather. "The music that I do is kind of the same stuff that Tim does," Jo Dee explains. "Tim and I have that in common."

It might sound trite, but hard work and determination elevated Tim from the status of an utter unknown, through talk that he would be just a one-hit wonder, to a position as one of Nashville's most respected young figures. Not only is he adored by millions of fans, he's also admired within the business he's gone all out to learn. Some of the lessons have been tough ones: Tim was sued by a former manager in 1993. Things can get nasty in the high-stakes music business, yet Tim remains one of the nicest, most easygoing guys you'd ever want to meet. The level of fame that Tim has reached is rare, and more than a few who've reached those heights have

> "I'm a student of this business. This is what I want to do. I might as well jump in with both feet."
> —TIM

wound up losing touch with what's real, but that simply can't be said of Tim McGraw.

Having landed two straight albums in the *Billboard* top ten, Tim was looking to take his work to another level. This was to be his most personal statement so far. "Before I even start looking for songs," Tim explains, "I have the sound in my head and this flow that I want to create with the album." He hasn't a fixed idea of using one specific type of song, but he tries to integrate different elements to create an overall mood to the album. It's easier said than done. In preparation for recording *Everywhere*, Byron and Tim sifted through some 500 submissions in their search for the perfect eleven songs to comprise Tim's fourth full-length release.

With that much quality material to pick through, some worthwhile compositions had to be left off. One of the songs that failed to make the cut on *Everywhere*, "It's All the Same to Me," was later snapped up by Billy Ray Cyrus, who released it as a single. It wasn't the first time that Tim had to pass on a fine tune. Back in 1993 he let "Nothing But the Wheel" slip by, and it went on to become a hit for Patty Loveless.

"The easiest thing in the world for me is to just be a regular guy. The hardest thing is when everyone expects me to be something other than that."

—TIM

> "It's important for me to find the right songs for my sound and style. But I also want to push the envelope and do things people don't necessarily expect."
>
> —TIM

"*Everywhere* is beyond incredible and establishes McGraw as the standard-bearer for country music in the second half of this decade."
—CHUCK ALY, *Music Row*

* * *

Everywhere sold over 225,000 copies its first week in the stores, second only to the Wu-Tang Clan, according to SoundScan. When all was said and done, *Everywhere* was one of the best-selling country releases of 1997, an album that debuted at number one and then spent eleven weeks in the top spot, more than any other country album for the year.

It isn't a coincidence that Tim's work has gotten better in direct proportion to how much of a hand he's had in the creation of his own albums. He's a fast learner with a great sense for what makes a top-notch song. *Everywhere* eventually went triple platinum, bringing his overall albums sold to well over 10 million, and the album boasts no less than five of the best singles of 1997.

The reviews, as usual, were mixed. The critic for *Entertainment Weekly* gave it a lower rating than she'd bestowed upon *All I Want*, then dismissed "It's Your Love" as "sentimental dreck." *Country America*, on the flip side, called it Tim's "best yet." A *People* review graded the album just a "C" and knocked the songs as "state-of-the-heart trifles." The *All-Music Guide* gives *Everywhere* a mere two-

> "I'm really proud of this album. I think it's the best work I've ever done. I love the sound and the songs—the whole thing."
>
> —TIM

and-a-half stars, below its rating of Tim's debut album, although the actual write-up is more flaccid than hostile. Tim doesn't get real shook up over what the music press thinks, at least not enough to stop doing what he does best. He sticks to what pleases his fans and satisfies his artistic goals.

If the truth be told, critics who didn't appreciate *Everywhere* have no business reviewing Tim McGraw's albums—or New Country in general, for that matter. If a writer doesn't have a positive outlook in regard to a particular subgenre of country music, such that the writer tends to downgrade that style's most popular artists and seminal albums, then said writer shouldn't be trusted with the task of reviewing those artists and albums. And yet, that seems to be the state of affairs in current music criticism. If a reviewer is an elitist who doesn't like what's on Young Country radio and scoffs at what millions of folks love, so be it. But a critic whose tastes de facto exclude popular music shouldn't be assigned to review albums that fall within the critic's prejudices.

From the opening fiddle notes of "Where

"I just deliver the songs. It's up to each person to find their own meaning."

—TIM

the Green Grass Grows," *Everywhere* is New Country at its finest. The hooks are strong and true, the arrangements are dynamic yet classic, the lyrics speak of a love affair with everyday living, and Tim's voice is like that of a good old friend dropping in for a cold beer or a hot coffee and some real conversation. Tim's voice has a vulnerable, heart-on-his-sleeve quality. It's hard not to feel a camaraderie with him when he sings a song like "For a Little While," in which he recalls the brief but happy time he spent with an old flame. You want to put a hand on his shoulder and say you understand the feeling.

It's been suggested that each of Tim's first three albums are inconsistent, with the best material outshining the weaker songs, but *Everywhere* suffers from no such problem. True, the singles are unforgettable, irresistible. But the alternate tracks are no less so. This is one of those albums that was meant for long drives on an open road, where the listener can live out each song in his or her mind. Tim told *Country Weekly*, "I was looking for that Eagles mid-tempo kind of feel," referring to the ultimate California Cool country-rock band of the 1970s.

The Eagles influence flows through the entire album, but nowhere more so than on the title song, where ex-Eagles bassist Timothy B. Schmit contributes backing vocals. Perhaps the least famous of the group's various members, as he didn't join the band until seven years after its inception, Schmit was cowriter and singer of the group's last top ten hit, the ballad "I Can't Tell You Why."

In joining the Eagles, Schmit stepped in for Randy Meisner, whose shoes he also filled back in 1970 for Poco, a country-rock band that formed from the ashes of Buffalo Springfield, the '60s folk-rock-country outfit that included Neil Young and Stephen Stills. Poco was a rock band with a strong streak of country; in fact, drummer George Grantham later settled in Nashville, first with Ricky Scaggs, then with Steve Wariner. He later reunited with ex-Poco pedal-steel guitarist Rusty Young for a tour with Vince Gill in 1984, for the debut of Vince's first solo mini-album. Vince had been a member of Pure Prairie League, yet another country-rock group Tim listened to as a teenager and whose influence shows up all over *Everywhere*.

The album has a couple of rave ups à la "Indian Outlaw" or "I Like It, I Love It"—

namely "Hard on the Ticker" and "You Turn
Me On." The latter, which is listed as a
"bonus song," could certainly have been a
single. The guitar breaks are blazing, the energy is sky high, and it sure sounds like Tim is
having a great time singing it. But most of the
songs on *Everywhere* are rooted in the "mid-
tempo Eagles" feel, with a dash of George
Strait ("Just to See You Smile," which spent
an incredible forty-two weeks on the *Billboard* chart) thrown in for good measure.
"Where the Green Grass Grows" may well be
Tim's favorite song from the album. "It re-
minds me of summertime and Little League
baseball," he explains. It was the first one he
picked for inclusion, it leads off the set, and it
was his pick for the initial single until Faith
Hill joined him on "It's Your Love."

Some might say that the most powerful
moments to be found on *Everywhere* are the
ballads, which cover an expanse of emotion.
The rapture of "It's Your Love" makes a clear
impact on those souls who aren't 100 percent
jaded. But the nonsingle "I Do but I Don't"
tells of the ambivalent side of love, the con-
flicted feelings that come when hearts are
bruised and unsure. It's a given that no one
will compare Tim's pipes to those of George

Jones—Tim himself has commented, "I'm not that much more talented than anybody else. There are people out there working at 7-Eleven stores that can sing circles around me"—but the spirit of George's work runs through Tim's performance of "I Do but I Don't." Having grown up not far from George's home in east Texas, Tim's young ears took in the sound of perhaps the finest vocalist in country music annals, and he couldn't help but be influenced.

Two of the biggest hits from the album are the melancholy title track and the sad but redemptive "One of These Days," a song that has a lot in common with *Not a Moment Too Soon*'s "Don't Take the Girl" in its tracing of a person's spiritual growth from child to adult. It isn't unusual for listeners to be brought to tears the first time they hear either song.

On the title track, "Everywhere," visions of a relationship left behind haunt Tim's mind, even as he understands that the decision to separate was right for both people in practical respects. Again, this is the most Eagles-esque tune on the album, with gentle acoustic and pedal-steel guitar melds, sentimental fiddle flourishes, and a simple, laid-back rhythm track. It's a superb example of what Tim brings to a song: nothing slick, no showing off, just honest interpretation. "I just try to sing it straight and show that I mean it," he explains. He lets the song speak for itself and in doing so puts an indelible personal stamp on it.

Everywhere drew high praise from Tim's peers in Nashville. Mila Mason lauded it as her favorite of the year. Rhett Atkins raved about the quality of the songs, commenting "You can tell a lot of thought went into selecting each and every one." Fans and radio consultants must've felt the same as Rhett and Mila. *Everywhere* churned out three number one singles: the title track, "It's Your Love," and "Just to See You Smile." The latter two spent six weeks apiece at the top of the *Billboard* country singles chart. No song had spent that long in the top spot since 1977, when Waylon Jennings scored with "Luckenbach, Texas," and Tim is the first artist since Buck Owens in the mid-'60s to turn the trick twice.

When nominations were announced for the 33rd ACM Awards, Tim was on the ballots in more categories than any other performer. Four of those were for "It's Your Love," which came in as a clean sweep for Tim and Faith.

The other two nominations were for Album of the Year, (which went to George Strait for *Carrying Your Love with Me*) and Entertainer of the Year (which was won by Garth Brooks). There could be no shame in taking four out of six, with the losses coming against the two biggest names in modern country.

The recognition and honors kept pouring in; Tim was a guest on the *Late Show with David Letterman* in August of 1998, and in late September he sang "Just to See You Smile" at the Country Music Association Awards show. His name was on the ballots in several major categories, including the coveted Entertainer of the Year, Male Vocalist of the Year, and Album of the Year. When the CMA nominations were first announced, Tim had commented, "I'm absolutely thrilled, and I am excited for my wife [who was also in the running for several awards]. It's a pretty good day for the McGraw household." As had been the case at the ACMs, Tim was in competition with the two reigning kings of country music. Garth again took home Entertainer, while George won Male Vocalist. But this time it was Tim McGraw whose name was called to collect the trophy for Album of the Year.

* * *

To those who know him, Tim has long been seen as a giving person, but his entry into the upper-income bracket and his initiation into fatherhood awakened new focus and options. Tim is fast becoming one of the most charitable and generous folks in Nashville. For example, he's had a soft spot in his heart for animals since childhood: He owns a farm outside of Nashville that is home to assorted dogs, ducks, horses, and cows. He wants his kids to have access to a good zoo because, in his view, it will help them to appreciate the creatures who share the planet with us. When the Nashville Zoo relocated to Grassmere Wildlife Park, Tim volunteered to perform to raise awareness and funds.

Tim has also turned his lifelong love of sports into a method of fund-raising for good causes. He participates in the annual City of Hope softball game, which is considered the unofficial start of Fan Fair week, to raise dollars for research on cancer and other diseases. Tim and Tug have at times joined forces for various charities, in conjunction with the Major League Baseball Players Alumni. Prior to one such event, Tug joked, "Tim's been

> "While I'm not going to run for mayor . . . whatever I can do to make Nashville a better place is all right with me."
>
> —TIM

"WOW! It all fell into place." —FAITH
(with Tim at the 1994 Country Radio Seminar)

"When I was in baseball I tried
to take it to an art form. I see Timmy
doing that with his music."
—Tug McGraw

"Go for it. Just do it. And don't let
anybody tell you you can't."
—FAITH

Celebrity/Paschal

"It's changed my life." —FAITH
(on fans' letters)

Celebrity/Scott

"This is the most rewarding thing that's ever happened to me in my life." —TIM (on his wife and children)

"I can't imagine how I can be so lucky." —TIM (with his mom, at the 1995 Fight Against Breast Cancer benefit)

Globe/Barrett

Celebrity/Ortega

"I'm a redneck and I admit it."
—TIM (at the 1995 American Music Awards
and, below, with Tracy Lawrence
and Bryan White)

Globe/Ryba

Faith with Loretta Lynn
at the 1995 Country Music Awards

Globe/Rose

Globe/Rose

"I'm sure glad I got that blonde
to sing with me. . . . " —Tim
(at the 1998 American Music Awards)

racking up the hits over the last couple of years. Let's see if he can get one off me this time." Tim shot back, "My hits come in a whole different area. I just hope to get the bat on the ball. It's hard to hit some of that junk he throws."

Tim tends to keep a low profile in his work for others. He believes in doing good deeds behind the scene, not for personal glory. But in at least one instance he improved two lives without even knowing it. In March of 1998 a report came across the wires: A Las Vegas radio station guarantees that there will be no repeat songs during the workday. One day they slipped up and played "Just to See You Smile" twice in a nine-to-five period. The couple who called in to collect $1,000 was in such dire financial straits that they were on the verge of pawning their wedding rings to raise cash.

Of course, that windfall was a fluke, but it can also serve as a reminder that music often has power that surpasses what the artist might expect, and that it operates in unusual ways. A musician sends songs out into the world as he would his children, cared for as best as can be but without guarantees, hoping they'll have some kind of positive effect.

PART TWO

❧ ❧

Faith Hill

"There are no overnight
sensations."

CHAPTER FOUR

Music for the Angels

"I was the loudest singer in the choir. Probably
not the best, but definitely the loudest."
—FAITH

Although she came into this world on the
twenty-first of September, 1967, in the city of
Jackson, Mississippi, Faith Hill's life began
in earnest about a week later, when she
was adopted by Edna and Ted Perry of tiny
Star, Mississippi. Both of Faith's parents had
longed for a little girl to join their sons, eight-
year-old Wesley and five-year-old Steve, but
Ted was still a little unsure when Edna urged
adopting a newborn. Already working hard to
make ends meet, the idea of a fifth mouth to
feed made him nervous.

But the first time he held his daughter in
his arms, Ted's resolve overcame his reticence,

and he knew that it would all work out for the best. The name Edna and Ted chose for the new addition, Audrey Faith, was an expression of their belief that God would grant them a baby girl, and it soon grew clear that this union was indeed kissed by the angels. Faith basked in the light of a happy and wholesome childhood, and Ted and Edna raised a daughter of whom they couldn't be more proud.

As a youngster Faith wasn't keen on her given name, wishing instead to be known by a more conventional one. With time she came to appreciate the love reflected in her mom and dad's choice, and to see her name as a sort of spiritual reminder. "I know there are roads laid out for me, and I just have to have faith I'll take the right one," she told Neil Pond of *Country America*. Of course those roads didn't take her on a direct route to where she is now—there were plenty of mistakes to be made and lessons to be learned along the way—but the one constant has been an unshaken trust that she'd find her place.

Almost from the time she could speak, Faith wanted to sing. She had music in her soul and a gift for expressing it that belied her years. It's been reported that she first performed in public at the tender age of three. "My mother said that I held the hymnal upside-down and sang as loud as I could, pretending I could read the words off the book," she has explained. She loved the rich and boisterous harmonies of the church choir, and her future musical direction was influenced by gospel songs she heard at the local Baptist church.

At age seven Faith sang for her 4-H club at a mother-daughter luncheon, but like most kids she was sometimes outgoing and other times shy. Whenever she was feeling reserved about singing for her relatives or friends of the family, Faith would accept pocket change from her mother in exchange for a song. A quarter was the going rate, but Faith asserts, "If it was a big family reunion it went up to fifty cents." Her repertoire featured then current hits such as "Delta Dawn," which was a smash for Tanya Tucker in 1972, as well as traditional fare such as "Jesus Loves Me."

Christian standards were the key aspect of Faith's musical upbringing. "The music in church was the first music I ever heard," she told Bob Paxman of Country Song Roundup. She started in the youth choir and was later allowed to perform with the adults when she was just sixteen. "That is a great place to start, and I learned a lot from those church groups," she has said. In the summer Faith would join the youth choir on singing trips around the region. Some of her favorite memories are of those times, and she explains that those trips were where she "cut my musical teeth."

Faith still cites "Peace in the Valley" as perhaps the song she cherishes most in the world. Later in life the powerful synergy of religion and music carried her to new places, when she toured with her first gospel group. At southern Baptist churches with large black congregations she found kinship in her passion for God and song. "People were on their feet the entire time at those churches," she remembers. She once told *CyberTalk*: "I wish country music had more black performers because of the diversity that it brings to the field and the soul is so deep. Just like the music that I grew up with in church." Years later, when Faith's church in Star was burned to the ground, she arranged a concert in Jackson to raise money for the rebuilding project.

Edna tried to see to it that Faith stayed in balance, whether she succeeded or failed.

"I think about the way my mother raised me. I turn the table around and see that she always told me, 'Just because you didn't win that race, or whatever, it's okay. I love you and that is all that really matters.' "

—FAITH

"My mom has always, always taught me to keep my feet on the ground in whatever I did. The things when I was in school, things that I won, or talent shows or whatever, to her it was most important that I kept my head screwed on straight." Faith's parents were strong in their faith, and they stressed to their children the prime tenet of Christian belief, the Golden Rule. "Mom always taught us not to be judgmental, to be honest, to put ourselves in someone's shoes," she recalls. Faith also learned a great deal about how to treat others from a young woman at church named Diane, whose kindness made a big impression on Faith as a youngster. Faith had strong adult role models as a child, many of whom were female. She grew up respecting herself and others.

The lessons weren't lost on Faith, who is one of the most compassionate and thoughtful people you could ever want to meet. She spends a ton of time and effort helping others and is especially committed to supporting and promoting charities that fight illiteracy. Teaching adults to read is an endeavor near and dear to Faith's heart, as her father, who was one of fourteen children in a poor family, never learned to read.

Ted Perry came from blue-collar roots and worked hard all his life. A fine husband and father, he accomplished much in his life. In a Father's Day article for *Country Weekly*, Faith told of how she would wait eagerly for him to come home from work each day. What makes the memory so special to her is that he never failed to come home; she could trust him to be there for her. She continued, "I've always had the comfort of having a dad who was there for me and still is—every step of the way."

Faith's parents offered her unconditional love and encouraged her to be herself. She led a well-rounded life, playing sports and loving the outdoors on one hand, and cheerleading and acting as scorekeeper for the boys' teams on the other. Faith did well enough in school but was never destined for a life in academics. Her favorite television show was *Little House on the Prairie*, which she considers required viewing for children. "I cry every time I see one of those shows. They teach you so much about morals," she proclaims.

Not that she was strictly a good girl who never tested the boundaries. A bit of the rebel was in her genes, and Faith was no delicate flower as a youngster. She hated to eat her vegetables, loved to jump in the mud, and would come home with hard-won scrapes and bruises from her efforts to keep up with her older brothers. Sure she wore frilly dresses for church, but then she'd come home, change clothes, and "get all dirty and yucky again." One time she was perched on the handlebars of her brother's bicycle when her foot caught in the spokes. The resulting tumble put her in the emergency room, but it didn't slow her down for long.

As she once told *Entertainment Weekly*, "I wasn't a hoodlum or anything, but I liked to get in trouble a little bit, to see how far I could go." It's a subject she would later tackle on her hit single "Wild One," a song her mom claims fits Faith to a tee. It's not hard to see why Edna Perry sees her daughter in the song, which in late 1993 became Faith's first chart-topper. It describes a "woman-child" whose dad told her as a little girl, "You can be anything you wanna be," and who winds up doing things her father never anticipated. Faith credits her parents with allowing her to "explore different things," while not letting their daughter "go rambling wild and crazy."

* * *

"I was very independent and when I
had my mind set on doing anything,
I thought I was going to do it."
—FAITH

The heroine in "Wild One" isn't tethered to tradition, and she isn't afraid to take the hard road. She also "loves rock 'n' roll" regardless of the protestations of her elders. That, too, might just as well be a description of Faith, who is far from fenced in when it comes to her listening habits. Her earliest and most important musical influence outside of church was Elvis Presley. She notes, "The first album I ever owned was Elvis's *A Legendary Performer Volume Two*." She also got to see him perform, in Jackson in 1975.

Sadly, by the time Faith and her peers were old enough to discover the King, he was in decline, having been dethroned artistically and commercially by the Beatles. But that's not to suggest his presence and his legacy didn't continue to loom over the musical landscape. Classics such as "Don't Be Cruel" and "Can't Help Falling in Love" were essential in forming Faith's conception of how music was supposed to feel, and how songs were to be interpreted by a vocal artist. In tandem with his rock and Vegas connections, which appealed to the "Wild Girl" in Faith, Elvis also had ties to both gospel and country music, which spoke to her traditional side.

* * *

"Oh, he's incredible. I had the biggest crush on him. . . ."
— FAITH on George Strait

Today's country doesn't get much more traditional than George Strait, and Faith is one of The Man's biggest fans. In high school she once talked her brother Steve into driving her all the way to Houston from Mississippi to see George Strait in concert. Faith recalls that the opening act was a local singer, a young girl not so much older than Faith. Big dreams running wild in her mind, Faith leaned over and told her brother, "I bet you one day I'm gonna open up for this guy." It's a good thing Steve didn't put down money against his sister, because years later she would, in fact, be an opener for George Strait.

High school wasn't as hard on Faith as it is on some people—she was once voted "Most Beautiful" and "Most Popular"—but that doesn't mean she didn't have insecurities. Still the solid foundation she had with her parents and church gave Faith strength when she needed it. In fact, it remains that way to this day. "I always fall back on my upbringing to get through tough times," she asserts. "My ultimate goal is to always have God as my pilot, whether it's in my career or my personal life."

About the time Faith entered McLaurin High School she became aware of the strong, independent female role models of country music. She lists among her favorites Amy Grant and Emmylou Harris, each of whom pushed the envelope within their respective genres: Grant in modern Christian music and Harris in country. Those are two of Faith's immediate predecessors, but her roots can be traced back to two legends:

Patsy Cline

"One of the greatest singers," according to Faith, the Hall of Fame vocalist's *12 Greatest Hits* was the all-time best-selling country album by a woman until Shania Twain scored with *The Woman in Me*. It is also the album Faith has at times listed as her all-time favorite. Patsy's recordings include the smash hits "Crazy," "I Fall to Pieces," "Walkin' After Midnight," and "Sweet Dreams." Brenda Lee, Kitty Wells, and Wanda Jackson were also important female artists from the 1960s, all of whom blazed the trails by which women are making extensive inroads into Nashville.

Tammy Wynette

Not only was Tammy's music a seminal influence, the Queen of Country also touched Faith's life in a personal respect. "I became friends with her and got to know the woman behind that great music," Faith was quoted in *Country Weekly*. Faith covered " 'Til I Can Make It on My Own" for the tribute compilation *Tammy Wynette . . . Remembered*. That song was one of four number one singles Tammy released in 1976 alone, and one of twenty she had during her incredible career.

At age seventeen or so Faith joined her first band, performing at rodeos, fairs, private parties, churches . . . wherever there was an audience. The situation came about after she took part in the Jimmie Rodgers festival in Meridian, Mississippi. The members of a band performing at the festival asked if she would join them, and she said yes. It was a cover band, doing the hits of George Strait and Reba McEntire and gospel standards—all the music that was special to Faith. She reflects on it now as a great learning experience.

Faith recalls that the strangest place she ever performed was in Raleigh, Mississippi,

> "I saw her show, and I knew right then and there what I was going to be doing for the rest of my life."
> —FAITH on Reba McEntire

as the entertainment portion of a "tobacco spit." Faith once explained in *People* that "they would set these spitoons at the end of the stage and the men and women, some with teeth, some without, would stand way back to see who could spit farthest into the spitoons. It was so gross. They had to clean the stage off with a towel before we played."

What her act lacked in refinement, Faith made up in unbridled enthusiasm. The flame of her desire to be a professional singer was glowing hotter and brighter than ever before, and the artist who had stoked that conflagration was a redheaded spitfire named Reba. At one point in her life Faith would have the chance to meet her idol, and she recalls of that moment, "I was totally speechless, but as I was walking away I just turned around and said, 'I love you, Reba McEntire!' And she said, 'I love you, too, honey.' "

Reba McEntire

The most successful and influential of the women of New Country, Reba got her start back in 1975 but hit it big in the mid-1980s with more than 20 million albums sold and over a dozen number one singles to her credit. Her hit "Is There Life Out There" became a personal anthem for many young women, and Reba has remained revered among her legion of fans in spite of the artistic twists and turns she's taken. Reba is, without doubt, the artist to whom Faith was most compared when she first appeared on the Nashville radar. In a write-up of Faith's second album, one reviewer commented that "her phrasing, pacing, and vocal color are often eerily reminiscent of [Reba]." The critic went on to conclude that *It Matters to Me* sounded like "the best little album that Reba never made. . . ."

In the cathartic "Is There Life Out There," a young woman wonders if she should leave home to take a chance on the unknown. As she entered the initial stage of adulthood Faith also faced such a choice. She had enrolled in junior college but wasn't focused on finishing school and getting a nine-to-five job. She wanted to be a country singer, but the pursuit of that dream required making a move to Nashville—no small step for a nineteen-year-old from Star.

This might be a scenario in which you'd picture the "Wild One" striking out on her

> "I remember coming home after school and playing her records in my room over and over until it was time for supper."
> —FAITH on Reba McEntire

own as her parents are left behind to wonder what went wrong. Yet in Faith's case the opposite is true: Ted and Edna helped their daughter pack her belongings into a small truck, then went so far as to briefly relocate to Nashville until their daughter could get her sea legs. It was a good thing, too; as she put it in *Country America*, "I wasn't mature enough to do this on my own when I first moved up here."

Faith's bond with her mother was always very deep and strong. Looking back on this time in her life, Faith remembers how her mom supported and encouraged her. Later, in a press release for her second album, Faith said of her mother, "I feel that it was real hard for her to let me go from the nest at such a young age. Now, the older I get, I think about having kids, and wonder if I'll be strong enough to let my daughter or son go and follow their dreams?"

It took a couple of months for her to find employment, but what she found would prove poetic. Faith's first job in Nashville was selling T-shirts at the Country Music Fan Fair. "I didn't know what Fan Fair was at the time," she has confessed, "but I do now." Indeed she does; in fact, in a neat twist of fate,

Faith is now one of the most popular singers at the same annual event where she once sold T-shirts.

Each spring since 1972 hard-core fans of country music have converged on Nashville's Fan Fair for fan-club get-togethers, autograph sessions, and concerts with the biggest stars in the business. It's a unique experience for all involved, and for an aspiring singer like Faith it was intoxicating. Watching the event unfold she told herself that if the time ever came when her name was on a booth at Fan Fair, she would remember how it was to be on the other side of the autograph table.

Of course, Fan Fair didn't last forever, so Faith had to hunt down other means of keeping food in her fridge. One job she landed—even more perfect than the Fan Fair gig—was with the fan club of her idol, Reba McEntire. It was exciting while it lasted, but soon Faith was on to other things. She believed that working in the office of a music executive might be the ticket to putting her singing career on track, so she sought a spot behind a desk on Music Row. Trouble was, Faith's open approach didn't fly in the business world. "Interviewers would always ask if I was a singer, writer, or had anything to do with music," she recounts. "I would say, 'Yeah, as a matter of fact, do you have a band I can play in? Do you know somebody?' "

After a couple of unrewarding interviews, it dawned on her that the companies had seen too many employees who were looking only for a stepping-stone to a stage career. It was best to keep her ambitions under her hat, and that's what she did. The new strategy paid off, and Faith was hired to greet people and answer phones at Gary Morris Music, a Nashville music publisher. She told them a little white lie, that she was in Nashville to go to college, not be a singer.

After a year or so of office work, she started to wonder about the path she'd taken. "I was in there thinking that I had definitely got myself into a bind," she said in a 1994 *Music City News* article. "I just sat back and watched everything happen, didn't say anything, and was dying inside. I was about to explode because that's not what I moved up here for—to sit behind a desk."

Being a receptionist wasn't her final goal, but at least she'd be around folks in the business, any one of whom might give her the break she needed. Plus, she was learning the tricks of the trade from the inside. "I got to see sides of the business that I never even thought existed," she would later tell *Country Music*. Faith is the first to admit that she was as green as a sapling, and she laughs when looking back at her mistaken assumption that the time listings for album tracks referred to the times of day in which the songs were recorded.

Faith's growth wasn't limited to business matters. She was working to make a life with Daniel Hill, a publishing executive to whom she had gotten married. She doesn't speak in-depth about the details of this period of her personal life, other than to note, "No beating or cheating occurred," and that she "felt captured." Faith had fallen in love at a tender age and taken a vow she would later have to break, but for the first five years of her life in Nashville she tried to make things work.

This was a period in which Faith learned a lot about herself, about what she feels and what she believes. She grew as a person and gained experience in reconciling other people's needs with her own, a theme that pops up in some of her songs, such as "Someone Else's Dream" and "I Can't Do That Anymore." She came to understand that it is

"I got married when I was very young and went through a lot of turmoil. Being brought up in a very perfect world, when you get married, you stay married. That didn't happen to me."

—FAITH

okay to make a mistake, that a mistake should be faced and put right if possible. She told Lahri Bond in *@Country*, "In my mind, whenever you admit something, then you're growing. You are finding yourself and becoming more comfortable with who you are. . . . That's how I like to live my life, period."

Faith's education as a singer came on a firsthand, learn-under-fire basis, too, and her fledgling career began to inch ahead, albeit a lot later than she'd pictured when she first hit town. Faith confesses that as a naive teenager she expected to "get on the Grand Ole Opry stage, start singing, and be on a bus traveling the next day." Instead it took the better part of six years for Faith to catch a break, and longer still to become the star she'd dreamed of being. She explained in 1995, "I have been in Nashville for eight years now. I had lived here five years before things started happening. Believe me there are no overnight sensations."

CHAPTER FIVE

Into the Light

> "Go for it. Just do it. And don't let anybody
> tell you you can't."
> —FAITH

One afternoon at Gary Morris Music, her patience was rewarded. Faith recalls, "David Chase heard me singing when I thought I was alone in the office and asked me to do a demo of a song called 'It Scares Me.' " Faith accepted the songwriter's offer and cut the demo. A couple of weeks later David played the tape for Gary Morris, who was impressed by what he heard. Although he knew he'd be losing a good worker, he had to encourage Faith to pursue singing as a career. He basically told her to get out from behind the desk, get out there, and get busy.

"That was a little kick I got from Gary and I took his advice from that point on," she recalls. Gary Morris wasn't the only Gary who helped give Faith's career "a little kick." She soon met and earned a spot as a backup vocalist for Gary Burr, an artist whom Faith credits with teaching her much about the finer points of stage presence, harmony, writing, "and pretty much everything." A superb songwriter, Burr would later contribute three songs to Faith's first album. Regular gigs at the Bluebird Cafe, a landmark local watering hole, were educational in the extreme. "Going out three or four nights a week—that's a school in itself, where you learn a good song from a great one," explains Faith.

Her knockout voice drew the attention of Warner Bros. A&R executive Martha Sharp, the talent scout who first signed Randy Travis. A couple of months after Martha heard Faith at the Bluebird, the two women met again, at a publishing company fish fry. Martha inquired as to whether Faith was "working a solo career." The two women discussed Faith's career plans. She later recalled, "Martha Sharp saw from the first meeting that I was pretty strong-headed and knew what I wanted."

* * *

> "That's where it all started, right there—a little eight-track tape. That's pretty cool!"
>
> —FAITH

It happens that Faith had put together an eight-track demo with Gary Burr, which they'd recorded in Gary's living room at home. Faith brought it to Martha, who liked what she heard and set the wheels in motion for Faith to receive a recording contract with Warner Bros. As reporter Robbie Woliver would later write in *New York Newsday*:

A gorgeous young country singer with strawberry blond hair, a confident voice that easily shifts from gritty to cotton-soft . . . wants a record deal. To top it off, she comes from a small southern town called Star.

Do you start counting royalties before or after she leaves your office?

On the evening of March 2, 1993, at the Warner/Reprise Nashville Superstars show for the Country Radio Seminar, Faith Hill made her debut as a major-label artist, performing in the same Grand Ole Opry auditorium where she'd imagined herself singing throughout her life. "I was just numb," she later confided to Craig Peters of *CountryBeat*. "And I was out there for two songs, walked off the stage, and I swear, I can't tell you anything about it! Except I saw WSM GRAND OLE OPRY, you know, on the microphone there, that's all I can remember! I was so nervous!" It was a dream come true to be sure, and she did savor the moment, but Faith knew that getting to the next level wasn't going to be easy, and that staying there would be even harder.

It was a roller-coaster time for Faith. The thrill of recording her debut album, *Take Me as I Am*, was tempered by her sadness over the breakup of her marriage to Daniel Hill. She decided to keep her last name, as her career was in full swing and she didn't want to cause confusion, but she just wasn't able to be happy within the confines of her marriage. Her friends could see it, Faith had to face it, and soon her parents had to hear the news as well.

In the wake of that turmoil, she kindled an intimate friendship with influential producer Scott Hendricks, who has worked with John Michael Montgomery, Brooks & Dunn, Aaron Tippin, Steve Wariner, and Alan Jackson. The heady blend of new freedom, new passion, and the flush of success put Faith in the right frame of mind for making a personal statement.

> "When I had to go to my mom and dad and say, 'I can't make this marriage work,' that was, to date, the most difficult thing I've ever had to do in my life."
>
> —FAITH

Record companies don't invest in artists whom they don't think have a chance to be huge. Why waste money and energy when there are so many hungry and talented wanna-bes waiting for an opportunity? With the backing of a major label came the possibility of stardom for Faith, but pressure was also part of the bargain. She would have to deliver a super album, work her tail off to promote it, and hope the radio stations got behind it. After that it would be up to the country music listeners to confirm or deny that Faith was worthy of the hype.

Released in the fall of 1993, *Take Me as I Am* is a time capsule of Faith's thoughts and feelings during an intense period of her life. She had a lot of sleepless nights, with a million ideas whiz-banging around her mind. Faith thought about all that had happened to her and what was to come. The record wasn't an instant smash—it didn't debut at number one or anything like that—but it was very well received by the press. A *People* reviewer called it "as enjoyable and promising a debut album as anything since Patty Loveless's 1988 rookie effort"—and it was perched on the cusp of *Billboard*'s top fifty by Christmas.

Not half bad for a first album, but the real splash was made with singles. Faith recalls the afternoon she first heard "Wild One" on the radio, in a car in Nashville. "It was incredible! I just cried, screamed and cried and screamed and cried!" she later revealed to *CountryBeat*. On the first day of 1994, Faith's first hit reached the top spot on the *Billboard* country singles chart. It was a roaring kick-start to the new year, and the party went into overtime as "Wild One" held its position for four weeks. Not since Connie Smith ("Once a Day," 1964) had a female artist posted a number one debut single for that long.

If scoring a number one is a home run, then keeping the top spot for four weeks is a grand slam. In an average year it happens two, maybe three times, and many years it doesn't happen at all. And to do it on her first swing . . . Faith had a tough act to follow—her own. A lot of folks would have become conservative with their next move, perhaps putting out a single similar to "Wild One," or at least not something from out of left field. But after talking it over with Scott, she decided to go for it with a pick that could be called the opposite of playing it safe.

"Critics, radio stations, Woodstock-era fans—they were like, 'Oh great. Here's this country crap singer trying to do this legendary song.'"
—Faith

In the summer of 1968 a San Francisco blues-rock ensemble, Big Brother & the Holding Company, cracked the top twenty on the pop charts with a song called "Piece of My Heart." Big Brother's lead singer was a young woman named Janis Joplin, and her pioneering vocal style and self-destructive lifestyle turned her into a rock legend after she died of a heroin overdose at age twenty-seven. Her biggest hit was a singular take on Kris Kristofferson's "Me and Bobby McGee," but "Piece of My Heart" has also long stood as a definitive Janis Joplin tune.

This was the song that Scott and Faith selected as the second single from *Take Me as I Am*—a Janis Joplin classic. Faith insists, "I'd never heard her version until I finished mine." In fact she had learned the song from a demo that James House has recorded in Nashville, done country style. Friends advised her not to listen to the original until she'd finished hers, "which turned out to be a great idea," explains Faith. She asserts that hearing it might have intimidated her out of making the attempt. "I couldn't have done it," she later confessed to *Headliner*. As it turns out, the long shot came in a big winner, as Faith's spirited interpretation of "Piece of

My Heart" hit number one at the end of April and soon went gold. "Those old rock 'n' rollers are now country music fans," Faith suggested.

Perhaps the most bantered issue in Music City is the absence of classic country on radio playlists. For her part, Faith laments that future generations are likely to grow up having never heard a Merle Haggard or Loretta Lynn song on the radio. She has said, "I hope we don't go so far that we forget about the legends that came before us." Faith is certainly part of the new wave of stars in Nashville who love old-fashioned country but are equally at home with classic rock; witness the heartfelt version of the Journey classic "Open Arms" that Faith often sings in concert.

Critics from both the rock and country camps were harsh toward Faith's take on "Piece of My Heart," with one calling it "stiff and soulless," and the others echoing that opinion. "I got crucified," Faith told Jeff Zaslow in *USA Weekend*. It's kind of amusing when you think about it. So often it seems the press responds to new music with a righteousness reminiscent of the preacher in *Inherit the Wind*, while fans listen to fresh sounds much as the kids in that same film are open to their science teacher's theories. The beat goes on, the music must change, and critics become less relevant with each snide comment.

With a pair of number ones under her belt, Faith was caught in a sudden whirlwind of attention. She was on a video of "Amazing Grace" for the feature film *Maverick*. Her duet with Brenda Lee on the children's song "Before You Grow" exposed Faith to a new audience of kids and moms—not to mention longtime Brenda Lee fans. And she made appearances on *Today* and *Late Night with David Letterman*, among other cable and network talk shows.

Most performers will admit that even if they've played in front of crowds their entire lives, appearing on television is disorienting. The lights and cameras, the distance between the live audience and the people on stage, and the sense of being rushed—all of it can create a sense of unreality in even the most grounded and experienced people. Faith has grown more sure of herself with time and experience, of course, and she was even tabbed to be on an episode of the TV series *Touched by an Angel*.

Music videos present another challenge,

but Faith has gone from tentative lip-syncher to confident visual performer over the course of her career. The director of her video for "Just to Hear You Say You Love Me," Jim Shea, says of Faith: "She's one of those people who comes to the party with her guns blaring. She has an intimate relationship with the camera and a powerful presence."

Television also has a distorting effect on the folks who are watching. It makes the stars seem larger than life. Faith recalls that after the first time she appeared on TV, her six-year-old nephew Jeffrey thought Faith had become "the richest person in the world." He dreamed up a laundry list of big-ticket gifts for her to give him for Christmas, including a car and a VCR. Faith also gets tons of mail from little girls who want to grow up to be like her, but she is quick to point out that her life isn't a movie, and that she is a normal person with problems and faults just like everyone else.

Faith hit the road in support of *Take Me as I Am*, covering just about all the states on a grueling 150-date tour. She also made trips to Canada and the United Kingdom for her first international exposure. She tried to make it back to her Nashville condo at least once every couple of weeks, just to wash her clothes and catch her breath. She was fond of her humble abode, its high ceilings and rooms full of sunlight.

But she also wished for a place in the country, with horses and pigs and wide-open spaces, where her parents could visit and feel at home. By late 1995 she would own just such a parcel of land, complete with a horse barn and a small stream cutting through the property. Faith and Scott would four-wheel around the acreage, talking over their plans for the home they would make there together.

Exciting as it was to be traveling the world, the best part of touring was opening for some of the most admired acts in the business, including Brooks & Dunn, Reba McEntire, John Michael Montgomery, and Alan Jackson. Faith built a strong rapport with Alan, who later put pen to paper for her on the song "I Can't Do That Anymore" for her second album.

Faith considers her road experiences to be among the most important of her life, and she cherishes the memories of moments such as when she was given a bag of biscuits for her weimaraner, Grant, by a group of fans. It's those small but personal gestures the fans make that are priceless, although Faith also never gets tired of receiving the usual bunches of roses while on stage.

On the other side of the coin, Faith has also experienced the cold reception new artists often get when opening for big stars. She knows how it feels to look out at the faces of someone else's fans and see no response. As the warm-up act for George Strait, she claims there were nights when she almost left the stage in tears, saying "I just couldn't get them."

Like most musicians Faith's motivation is the pleasure of singing and of touching people with her music. Her fans showered her with acceptance and affection, and she felt humbled and thankful. She'd had—and would continue to have—her share of ups and downs. Most performers know how it feels to strive and fail, to not be able to connect with a particular audience. Truth be told, it's hard on the ego. But the cliché about country fans still holds: They're the most loyal in the world.

There's a special place in Faith's heart for her youngest fans, due both to her love of children and to the fact that their devotion is so pure and true. "They're standing up there with their little arms just stretched as far as they can possibly go! It's why we do this," she confided to Marianne Horner in *Country-Beat*. It doesn't happen every night, but there've been times when Faith would bring an enthusiastic young fan on stage to sing with her. The first time she ever did it was very special to Faith, as the moment was totally spontaneous.

Faith recognized each performance as a chance to reach people unfamiliar with her, so she rarely said no to an opportunity. One time she sang the National Anthem prior to a Dallas Cowboys game. Somehow a rumor sprang up that she'd forged a romantic link with Dallas quarterback Troy Aikman, a notion both Faith and Troy flatly denied. "I've heard every rumor you can imagine about me and Troy Aikman, but no, I don't even know him," she said when the talk first began.

The media pounced at the prospect of a star athlete and a beautiful singer dating each other, and things got so out of hand that at one point Troy contacted Faith's boyfriend Scott to assure him that the rumors were untrue. Troy offered Scott tickets to the Super Bowl as a gesture of goodwill, and Scott accepted. Soon enough the rumors stopped circulating and were more or less forgotten. Faith and Troy, by the way, did become friends in the wake of the speculation about their supposed relationship.

It was clear from Faith's comments in interviews during this period that she had deep feelings for Scott Hendricks, and that nothing transient was going to come between them. In interviews she spoke of a "special person" she hoped would ask for her hand in marriage. Those who were close to Scott saw that he, too, was head over heels in love with Faith. "She makes everyone around her feel good," he was quoted in a 1995 *People* feature titled "The 50 Most Beautiful People in the World." It wasn't easy for either of them when Faith was on the road and Scott was in the studio, but their relationship appeared to be moving ahead at a rapid clip.

Faith's next single, "But I Will," didn't do as well as her first two, topping out at thirty-five on the *Billboard* country singles chart. A tender portrait of a woman standing up to a cheating man and telling him she'll leave him even though she loves him, it was a change of

"I'll turn on the radio—this is no lie—and they'll be saying things like, 'Troy flew Faith to the Super Bowl; I wonder what he got her for Valentine's Day.' And I'm thinking, 'What? He didn't get me anything!'"
—FAITH

pace from "Wild One" and "Piece of My Heart," and a reflection of Faith's vocal abilities in the area of classic ballads.

Yet the fact that "But I Will" was just a modest success in comparison to Faith's first two singles meant that her next release would be more upbeat. The title track, "Take Me as I Am," fit the bill, and indeed it shot into second position on the *Billboard* chart before stalling. This made it two number ones and a near miss for Faith's debut album, and that was enough to elevate *Take Me as I Am* to a platinum plateau (one million sold).

Faith's peers didn't fail to notice her hard work and incredible potential. The Academy of Country Music tabbed her as the New Female Vocalist of the Year for 1993. In the past that honor had gone to artists who then went on to have full careers, such as Crystal Gayle and Trisha Yearwood. But other years it had gone to singers who weren't around for long at all. The award was not a guarantee of future success, but it was a sign that Faith had gotten off to a great start.

Then disaster struck. Months of nonstop singing and speaking had put immense strain on her vocal cords. She'd never received

"It's a long way from Oklahoma
and Louisiana and Mississippi up to
that ACM stage. . . . It's a long trip,
but it's possible."
—FAITH

much formal training as a singer, and she tended to let loose from her throat, rather than from her abdomen. What's more, she often failed to care for her voice as if it were a delicate instrument. In high school she had cheered and screamed at football games in the Mississippi heat and humidity. She'd attended rodeos where there was a lot of dust in the air.

Since moving to Nashville she had spent too many nights performing in smoke-filled bars and dance halls—the type of atmosphere that adds character if you're Willie Nelson but can end your career if you're Faith Hill. Since the release of her first album, she'd done hundreds of interviews, not wanting to turn down a single chance to show country music fans the person behind the music. "I just didn't get it. I thought there was no way all that talking could hurt me," she later confessed.

When she'd started moving in Nashville music circles, meeting a few of the established country stars for the first time, Faith had been given two pieces of good advice: Smell the roses and don't neglect your health. She had tried not to miss a single "rose," but that meant pushing her health to the limit. It was all too much—something had to give—and in the end a blood vessel in Faith's throat became enlarged, causing her to lose her stock in trade.

She could joke about it later, but when the trauma was diagnosed, she wasn't laughing at all; in fact, she was "scared to death." After surgeons at Vanderbilt University Voice Center operated on her throat, Faith still had to refrain from speaking for two weeks, and she was forced to take a full three months off to recover. While she was healing, Faith ate plenty of her mother's homemade chicken soup. She used the time off to collect her thoughts, take a break from the maelstrom of the music business. On the downside Faith was forced to bow out of concert commitments with George Strait and Alan Jackson.

Something else happened during Faith's time of silence: On Valentine's Day, Scott asked her for her hand in marriage. He told her to nod yes or no since she couldn't speak, and she indicated that, yes, she would be his wife. The happy pair didn't get very specific with the press about their wedding plans,

"For a big talker like me, that was a huge problem."
—FAITH

other than to confirm the good news to reporters, but it seemed that the engagement would last at least through Faith's next tour.

CHAPTER SIX

What Matters Most

> "I've gotten to do things that some artists never
> get to do in their career . . . but I don't think
> I'm there yet. I don't think I can honestly say
> that I'm secure in saying that I've made it."
> —FAITH

With wedding vows seemingly in their future, and Faith's voice at full strength, the newly engaged Scott and Faith ventured into the studio to record Faith's next album, *It Matters to Me*. Faith felt a level of pressure she hadn't suffered during the production of her first album. Sure, she'd been nervous then, but now she was up against the raised expectations of her record label, the fans, and herself. Faith made no secret of the fact that she was feeling the eyes and ears on her, "big time."

Sophomore expectations aside, she was also anxious to find out how her throat would respond to the demands of singing all day in the studio. Her surgeon, Dr. Robert Ossoff, had assured her that all was well, but she couldn't be certain until she put her vocal cords to the test. She practiced vocal exercises, which she had learned in speech therapy, to warm up before stepping to the microphone. But when the test came, she would either fly or fall.

Not only did her voice pass muster, if anything, it sounded even more gorgeous than it had prior to her going under the knife. Faith had risen above the weight of expectations and created a dead-on follow-up to *Take Me as I Am*. Her excellent debut had been a declaration of arrival, but *It Matters to Me* proclaimed that Faith Hill was in it for the long haul.

It Matters to Me would go on to duplicate the double-platinum success of Faith's debut, but had it fallen short in the sales arena, Faith could still have been proud. From the opening song, "Someone Else's Dream," it is clear that she's coming into her own, both as a singer and as a person. And, in fact, she had covered a lot of personal and professional ground since leaving Mississippi, and much of it is chronicled in her second album. A reviewer in *People* enthused, "This album confirms that when it comes to country music, this Mississippi native-daughter is right at home."

One unexpected benefit of Faith's vocal problems was that she had extra time to search for new material. Faith and Scott sifted through hundreds of songs to find the final ten, among them one called "Roadkill," a song about a dead possum. Faith told a *People* reporter that she considered putting such a song in her live act just to see if her fans were listening. She elected not to put "Roadkill" on *It Matters to Me*, however, instead picking songs "that hit me the hardest, make me feel the most." Faith and Scott took the difficult process through several stages—the top fifty, the top twenty, and so forth—before settling on the right ones.

Like all Nashville singers Faith has an abiding respect for songwriters, but it isn't a challenge she is driven to take on. "It's a craft and a gift that needs to be fostered every single day," she has said, "and there are other things I want to do." Although she didn't write any of the cuts herself—"I was too lazy," she jokingly explained in *Country Song*

"I guess you could say I like diversity."
—FAITH

Roundup—each one exhibits a different aspect of Faith's artistic range.

"We put a lot of heart and soul and passion into finding each one of the songs that are on the record," Faith proclaimed. It would be tough to call any one of the ten tracks nonessential, as each is unique. "You Will Be Mine," for example, shows Faith's bluesier side, as she stakes a claim on the man she wants. It wasn't clear to her that she'd be able to pull off such a rockin' song, but once she got into the studio, it worked out without a hitch.

On the opposite side of the emotional spectrum, "A Man's Home Is His Castle" is a chilling tale of domestic abuse. Martha Sharp, the A&R rep who "discovered" Faith, brought this song to her, saying, "You've got to hear it." Faith listened to the cassette in her car, and she recalls the effect it had: "I was driving down West End in Nashville, and it really impacted me. I mean, I couldn't even tell there were cars around me. . . . I thought, 'My God. The pain and desperation and fight for survival that this woman is going through. . . .' " Faith's intense approach to music is reflected in her comments about this song to Bill Hobbs in *New Country*:

I don't care what people say. I don't care if they compare—"Oh, everyone's doing an abuse song now." I don't care. The bottom line is this song moved me. This song ripped my heart out when I heard it. This song speaks for itself.

Faith also pours her soul into "I Can't Do That Anymore," a knockout of a song that tells of a woman who is tired of trying to fulfill her husband's image of what she should be. Alan Jackson had promised to compose a song for Faith, and he had come up with an upbeat number that Faith thought was good but not what she'd had in mind. "Imagine me telling Alan Jackson that. I was just sick about having to tell him. . . ."

Alan went back to the drawing board determined to blow Faith's mind, and that's what he did. "I wrote you another song 'cause you pissed me off," Faith reports that Alan told her. She went out to hear the song during a sound check. Sitting with her steel guitarist, Gary Carter, Faith turned to him and said, "My Lord! I can't believe a man wrote that song." Alan humbly told Faith she could have the song if she wanted it, and, of course, she jumped at the offer.

Of course, some of the songs were put out as singles, and, as had been the case with *Take Me as I Am*, three tunes from *It Matters to Me* cracked the *Billboard* top five. The first to be released was the upbeat and romantic "Let's Go to Vegas," a melodic romp with clever lyrics, a locomotive backbeat, and slick steel-guitar work. "Vegas" belies the overall tone of the album, which is somewhat more serious and introspective than *Take Me as I Am*.

The second single from *It Matters to Me*, the title track, is a straight shot to the heart. No surprise, "It Matters to Me" soared to the top of the charts, then held that position for three weeks in the first month of 1996, thanks to a powerful chorus hook and Faith's sincere, graceful phrasing. Surprisingly, her first reaction when the song was pitched to her wasn't warm. Faith suspected she might have a hard time singing it, but Scott assured her it would go well, and the results speak for themselves. This became one of Faith's favorites, especially when performing live.

The third and final single was "Someone Else's Dream," which climbed to third on the *Billboard* chart, giving Faith a remarkable half a dozen top-five hits over the course of her first two albums. The character in "Dream" could be seen as the older sister to "Wild One," or perhaps the "Wild One" herself, ten years down the road, if she didn't stick to her guns. The woman in "Dream" has failed to take her own path, but there's still hope she'll locate the "Wild One" inside her. In a press release Faith said that the song is about "living your life according to everyone else's expectations, and then something happens and you suddenly go, 'Wait a minute! This isn't how I am at all, and I am about to show my true colors. I am now awake. . . .' It is like being born again."

It Matters to Me closes on an uplifting note with a gospel song that hearkens to Faith's days of singing with the Baptist church choir in Star. "Keep Walkin' On" was cowritten by Karen Staley, who also penned "Let's Go to Vegas," in addition to singing harmony and playing guitar with Faith's stage band. Karen had put out an album of her own in the mid-1980s, and this song was on it. "I just wanted the listener to be left with the positive message that this is what I believe and this is how I keep going every day," Faith professed.

"Keep Walkin' On" features vocals by Shelby Lynne, one of Faith's favorite singers.

The duo performed the song at the 1995 CMA Awards presentation, and the buzz in the Opry House indicated Shelby and Faith had just about stolen the show. "I could have let Shelby just sit there and sing the whole song by herself and that would have been fine with me," Faith said in deference, "but we had a great time."

In support of *It Matters to Me*, Faith once again took to the tour circuit as an opener for Alan Jackson. Asked by Kimmy Wix of *Music City News* how she felt about playing live at this juncture of her career, Faith responded, "I just feel a lot more comfortable and confident in my performing abilities onstage, and how I guide a show and carry myself."

Faith and her crew began calling their schedule the Book of Lies, as it seemed subject to constant revision. Putting together a major music tour takes an awesome amount of planning and hard work. Road crews for major artists often work together for years, becoming well-oiled machines. For the artists it isn't just a matter of plugging in and cutting loose at showtime. Pressure, frustration, and adjustment are all part and parcel of the pre-event scenario.

Faith is the good-hearted, sweet person she

appears to be, but she's also an exacting professional, a perfectionist at heart. She is involved in the steps of the recording process: picking songs, listening to new arrangements on her DAT deck—she even has a coproducer credit on *Faith*. It isn't much different on the road, where she is the leader of her band, a role she takes seriously. Not that she doesn't have a sense of humor about life's mishaps, but the chaotic nature of touring can wear on her.

She still gets nervous even under the best of circumstances. She told Michael Bane of *Country Music*, "I'm scared for my life the moment I walk on stage." When things go wrong with her equipment or her band, which is bound to happen at least once in a while, she sometimes hits the point at which, as she put it in *New Country*, "we're gonna kill each other . . . or . . . we're gonna be okay."

According to Faith, one of the things she learned from being in the music business is not to take things too seriously. When the stress level is high, Faith seeks solace in small things; for instance, finding a simple roadside stand and picking up some homegrown vegetables, then cooking a dinner of green beans, new potatoes, corn on the cob, and grilled chicken for her band.

Faith has learned a lot about cooking from her mom, who is a wiz in the kitchen. Faith also makes a mean lasagna, great meat loaf, and a chilled dessert called Fluffy Delight that includes pistachio instant pudding, crushed pineapple, Cool Whip, mini-marshmallows, and chopped pecans. Faith loves to fix dinners for her friends, and she often spoke with the late Tammy Wynette about getting together to cook, although sadly they were never able to follow through on the idea.

Faith loves food almost as much as she loves music—the enthusiasm oozes when she talks about her favorite brand of mayonnaise or her beloved tomato sandwiches (white bread and tomato slices). For instance, after waking up from throat surgery the first thing she asked for was something to eat, and her mom had soup at the ready. "I eat everything I'm not supposed to eat," Faith claims, but she also drinks gallons of water and gets a lot of exercise being on tour and chasing after her daughters.

In addition, Faith has a high metabolism that keeps her from putting on excess pounds;

in fact, she's sensitive about people referring to her as "skinny." She sees it as comparable to calling an overweight person "fat." The ladies in the lunchroom at school used to tell her, "Girl, eat some food!" As a teenager she had "a real complex" about her body type. "I was scrawny" is how she explained it in a *Country America* article titled "The 10 Most Fascinating Women in Country Music."

One of the best things about Nashville in the nineties is that such an article has more than enough eligible candidates for inclusion. If it used to be that radio programmers could all but ignore female artists, that's no longer the case. Never before has there been such an influx of women on the charts and airwaves. LeAnn Rimes, Terri Clark, Martina McBride, the Dixie Chicks, Jo Dee Messina, Deana Carter, Reba McEntire, Patty Loveless, Lila McCann, the Lynns, the Kinleys, Shania Twain, Trisha Yearwood are just a few of the women who've swept into Music City like a tidal wave.

All of the artists mentioned above would be the first to voice thanks to the women who threw open the gates, in particular Dolly Parton and Reba McEntire. Both had the talent and courage to take hold of the reigns of their own careers and succeed against the odds. Faith has commented, "Reba has shown that you can be in control of your business and still have your creative side. Dolly Parton's done the same thing, and they're both great examples for us."

For a time before she was discovered, Faith worked for the Reba-founded Starstruck Management, an experience Faith credits with teaching her invaluable business lessons. After her own solo career began to make a splash, Faith was involved in even the smallest aspects of her career. "There's not a decision that's made without me," she once affirmed to *Cross Country Music*. Of course, she was surrounded with experts and specialists in various areas—accounting, scheduling, design, etc.—but all the decisions that concerned her were made as a team, down to the smallest detail. She has even been involved in the design conception for her stage clothes, in addition to doing her own makeup.

So-called "women's issues," which by all rights ought to be everyone's concerns, have long been a major part of Faith's live agenda. She sings about women trapped ("I Can't Do That Anymore"), women in trouble ("A Man's Home Is His Castle"), and women being strong (her inspiring cover of Aretha Franklin's "Do Right Woman, Do Right Man"). In this respect Faith follows her idol, Reba, about whom she says, "I want twenty years from now to feel like I made a difference in people's lives, the way she did with 'Is There Life Out There,' sending people back to college." From the mail she gets, Faith is reassured that her songs touch other people's lives exactly as she hopes.

Faith has a response for programmers who balk at scheduling back-to-back songs by women: "You've gotta play those females. We are competitive—and that's a fact." Sentiments such as that one reflect a permanent change in the landscape. Women no longer have to *ask* for consideration based on vague ideas about equality. Instead they *expect* a fair shake based on the indisputable proof that they have what it takes. To ignore such a sea change is to risk being washed off the map.

Critics often rail about "packaged" artists who are spawned from the evil minds of record executives. These singers supposedly have the looks and the style and little else. Such animals may well exist, and Faith could be mistaken for one at a superficial glance:

She's breathtaking and charming, with a voice that sounds too good to be true on recordings. But if you hear her tear it up on-stage, you know her talent is genuine. And as for the physical appearance question, she points out, "There are a lot of good-looking people who didn't last very long because there wasn't any substance there. There was just a look. And that's what models are for."

Ultimately it's the record buyers, concert-goers, and radio listeners who cast the final vote on which artists are pretenders and which are the real deal. According to *TV Guide*, 58 percent of country album purchases are made by women. It's still the music that matters. Faith explains, "If the music is there, then you get past the looks and the clothes and all that—quickly." The numbers reveal that women are a force in Nashville, but it doesn't take a sales chart to prove the fact. All you have to do is go to a show and talk to the fans.

It isn't a platitude to state that Faith Hill has some of the most dedicated fans around. Whether standing in the sweltering sun or the pouring rain at an outdoor show, waiting without complaint during long delays when

"Then there are fans that write me letters and give them to me at the show. I read them when I get back on the bus. It's changed my life."
—FAITH

equipment breaks down, or lingering outside an arena for an autograph, Faith's fans have found a million ways to express their devotion. "If they feel you are sincere, and that you are their friend, the waters run very deep," she has said of her fans and of country fans in general. Faith used to receive a few shouted-out marriage proposals at each concert, although that has died down since she married Tim.

Some of her best fans have followed her tours through multiple cities, and others have come thousands of miles to see her at Fan Fair. During the week of Fan Fair, most artists throw a party for their fan club members. One year Faith had a skating party so that she could see her biggest fans up close, one-on-one. As a girl Faith used to spend a lot of time at the roller rink, and both her brothers worked there at one time or another.

When she first hit the big time Faith had to contend with a strange aspect of fame: going to a store or a mall and feeling the eyes on her, hearing whispers, but not being approached. Of course, the people were being polite, giving her the space to be a regular person. Yet the thing that made her feel uncomfortable

"When I'm not on the road, I go out in sweats with my hair up, like a hag. People come up to me and tell me I look like Faith Hill."

—FAITH

was being treated as if she were unapproachable. Contrary to what folks might suppose, Faith is open to her fans; she's flattered when they take the time and make the effort to reach out.

Faith is thankful for the love her fans have given her, in particular during the months she was recuperating from her throat operation. "I received so many cards, flowers, and gifts from friends, family, and fans," she explained. "I truly believe all the well-wishes made things more bearable." Faith understands it's crucial to "give back" to the less fortunate, and she gets involved with nonprofit events whenever possible. Children's charities hold a special importance for her.

An avid NASCAR auto-racing fan, Faith has been an integral component in the "race for diabetes." Mark Collie, one of Nashville's most respected singer-songwriters, is diabetic, and he helped put together a racing event to raise money and awareness about the disease. Faith and a host of other country stars have chipped in to make it an annual success.

"I'm a sucker for kids!"
—FAITH

PART THREE

∽ ∾

Tim & Faith

"They're definitely in love."

CHAPTER SEVEN

Burnin' Love

"Tim and Faith . . . have really been on a
roll this past year. To me, it seems like their
time has come."
—JOE DIFFIE

On March 14, 1996, in Wheeling, West Virginia, Tim and Faith started what would soon become one of the most famous concert tours in Nashville lore: the Spontaneous Combustion tour. Before it was done, this would be one of the top-grossing tours of the year, having been seen by more than one million fans in almost every state in the nation. But what made it truly special is that all those people bore testament to the blossoming of one of the sweetest, most spontaneous romances that country music has ever seen.

Tim and Faith had met twice before, first at a radio seminar in 1994, and again in 1995 when they both were performing at an outdoor music festival in Eau Claire, Wisconsin. In neither instance were they able to spend time getting to know each other, but Tim certainly noticed Faith. "I thought she was gorgeous, but out of my league," Tim has since been quoted.

When the Spontaneous Combustion tour kicked off, Faith was engaged to Scott Hendricks, who was, at the time, president of Capitol Nashville, the label whose stable of artists includes Garth Brooks. Even though Faith was on the Warner Bros. label, Scott had continued as her coproducer. On the liner notes for *It Matters to Me*, Faith wrote: "Scott, you have taught me patience and understanding, but most of all you have taught me love."

Sadly for Scott the forces of distance, circumstance, chemistry, and fate conspired to push him out of the picture. Tim and Faith were spending more and more time together offstage—cooking, going to movies, and getting to know each other. At a party in Nashville's fabled Two Rivers Mansion honoring Tim for his number one single "She Never Lets It Go to Her Heart," it was clear to all present that Faith had let Tim go to her heart.

The cold, hard truth is that Tim and Faith had grown to be more than friends, and Scott was left behind.

Letters began pouring into the offices of country music magazines; the phone rang off the hook at Tim's and Faith's fan clubs. Folks all wanted to get the inside scoop on country's hot new couple. In November of 1996 *Modern Screen's Country Music* ran photographs of Tim and Faith kissing onstage, along with an editorial note that read: "Faith recently broke off her engagement to Scott and, at press time, has been linked romantically with Tim McGraw, who recently broke off his engagement as well."

Rumor had it they were already married, and/or Faith was pregnant. Tim's mother, Betty Trimble, confirmed in *Country Weekly*, "They're dating, but it's nothing beyond that right now." Betty added, "I know I wouldn't mind if it went further because I think they make each other happy and I really like Faith."

Faith was slotted as the opener with Tim in the headlining role, although they could for all intents have been considered coheadliners. On a typical evening she kicked off her show on a soulful note with a blues-tinged "Someone Else's Dream." She has the vocal power and raw energy to lift listeners into the stratosphere, and the onstage manner that puts an audience at ease.

She might invite a child or two to join her for a song and a dance on "You Can't Lose Me." Plenty of outfit changes were on tap, from ripped jeans and a T-shirt to a tight fulllength dress. Karen Staley had left the band to work on a solo album, and new backup singer Lisa Gregg stepped into the spotlight to do "The Way You Do the Things You Do." It was a full show, more than enough to hold the attention of fans who might have at first considered Tim McGraw the main attraction.

Each night during the tour Faith would return to the stage about three-quarters of the way through Tim's set. She would join him on "Nobody Knows," an R&B song originally done by the Tony Rich Project. Tim and Faith would slow dance in each other's arms. He doesn't consider himself much of a dancer, but Faith sure didn't seem to mind, especially when they sealed the song with a kiss as the lights went down. That move let the captivated fans know there was more to the intensity on stage than mere show—there was real passion. Huge video screens captured the look of love in both their eyes.

A year and a half later Faith would tell Richard McVey II in *Music City News*, "We became very attracted to each other. We grew up in similar towns. His friends could have been from my hometown and vice versa. We were also alike in the way we wanted to raise our family."

One evening in Montana, before he went onstage, Tim popped the question. Faith was taken by surprise. She told him, "I can't believe you're asking me to marry you in a trailer house," which was the structure that served as Tim's dressing room. He slyly replied, "Well, we're country singers, what do you expect?" Faith didn't give an answer right away, but when Tim returned to his dressing room after the show, he found a message scrawled on the mirror: I'M GOING TO BE YOUR WIFE. YES, F.

One of Tim's tour dates was in his home area of northeast Louisiana, where he puts on an annual benefit for the community where he was raised. The event has been dubbed "Swampstock," a wordplay that combines the '60s music festival Woodstock and the local bayou geography. The first two Swampstocks had raised $90,000 for local baseball diamonds and scholarships, and this one raised $70,000 more. It was on October 6, intermixed with the charity softball game and the concert, that Tim and Faith took their vows in Rayville, Louisiana, the town where Tim's mom once worked as a waitress at the local bus stop café. That evening onstage Tim stopped the show to introduce his new bride to the thrilled and stunned audience.

The event had been kept on the q.t., so much so that the Dancehall Doctors didn't even know they were at a wedding until it started. They came dressed in softball outfits, under the mistaken impression that the gathering was for a pregame brunch in Tim's aunt's backyard. The witnessing of the vows was limited to a few close friends and family members, and in the following hours, the 70-odd guests managed to keep the secret until Tim could announce it on stage.

It was an idyllic day for a wedding, with sunny skies and mild temperatures, and the ceremony itself was simple and beautiful. A live chamber music ensemble played, and the yard was filled with flower arrangements. Faith and Tim were married by the Reverend Adrian Pater at noon under an oak tree, with two of Tim and Faith's old friends acting as best man and bridesmaid. A barefoot Faith wore a white dress and veil, while Tim was dressed in blue jeans and a long black jacket.

As the Spontaneous Combustion tour drew toward conclusion, so did the year 1996. The last show was at the new Nashville Arena in downtown Music City on New Year's Eve. It was the very first concert in the new venue's history, and it raised money for the Country Music Hall of Fame relocation fund. Tim and Faith sang in the new year together, holding hands and looking into each other's eyes. Every person in the arena could see and hear that it was true love, and it figured that some very special things were bound to come of it.

Faith had often joined Tim onstage to sing a song that he'd gotten from songwriter Stephony Smith. It hadn't appeared on a record yet, but Tim had plans to include it on his next release. The song, of course, was "It's Your Love," and when Tim and Faith did their smoldering version of it at the close of his shows, audiences were swept off their collective feet. "The response of the fans to this song live was the major reason behind releasing it as a single," Tim later asserted.

About a week before the mixing process

"I'm sure glad I got that blonde to sing with me on that."
—TIM

was begun on *Everywhere*, Tim asked Faith if she would provide supporting vocals on the recorded version of "It's Your Love." She agreed, and when the time came she joined Tim, James Stroud, and Byron Gallimore in the studio. But being seven months pregnant at the time, doing her part required about as much exertion as she could handle. Faith "could barely catch her breath," Tim recalls. Yet when she'd finished singing, it was Tim, James, and Byron who were left breathless. Everyone in the studio that day felt that something special had happened, and there was the shared sense that they had a real hit on their hands. "Afterwards, we all looked at each other and just felt like we had some magic there," remembers Tim.

At the 32nd Academy of Country Music Awards ceremonies in the spring of 1997, Tim and Faith performed "It's Your Love" and touched off a shockwave that would eventually make it the biggest hit of Tim's career. (The song isn't a duet in the traditional sense of the word, as Faith simply adds backup harmonies rather than singing any of the verses, so it appears on most charts as a Tim McGraw song. Otherwise it would rate as the bestseller of either artist's career.)

From then on it was the song that came to

mind whenever fans thought of Tim and Faith. There had been (and still are) times when Faith wasn't available to sing the song with Tim in concert, so he'd perform a sparse acoustic version with a member of his band doing the backing vocals. Now the audiences invariably sing along with him in sweet tribute, a lovely experience to say the least.

"It's Your Love" reigned on the charts for the rest of the year, and it dominated the radio and video airwaves. The song was just too good to remain exclusively on the country charts, and it soon crossed over to become a smash on all-genres lists as well. "It's Your Love" would eventually be nominated for two Grammies: Best Country Vocal Collaboration and Best Country Song.

Gracie Katherine McGraw was born on May 5, 1997, at 8:12 A.M., three and a half weeks early and weighing 4 pounds 14 ounces. Mother and daughter left the hospital on schedule, and as the proud parents were exiting the hospital with Gracie, Faith joked, "Do you think they realize that they just let us walk out of the hospital with a baby." All kidding aside, Faith is "a natural at being a mother," according to Tim, and Faith confirms

"And then when Tim and I found each other, we fell in love and married and had a beautiful daughter, it was just like, Wow! It all fell into place."

—FAITH

that Tim is an ideal father, too. That fact is evident is his actions and his words. "Now everything I have is for them," he asserts.

Gracie gave both Tim and Faith a focal point for their lives, a reason not to fret about the little things and to get down to the business of building a strong foundation for their child and her future siblings. Faith is adamant about the fact that she no longer sweats all the minutiae that used to drive her to distraction. As she explained to Michael Bane in *Country Music*, "I don't have time!"

In late September of 1997, at the 31st Country Music Association Awards, "It's Your Love" was voted Vocal Event of the Year, ahead of duets by, among others, Clint Black and Martina McBride, and George Jones and Kathy Mattea. It was a great honor, no doubt, but nevertheless just a precursor to the one that was in store at the ACM Awards a few months later.

A year after it had been debuted for a national audience, "It's Your Love" was up for trophies in four categories at the 33rd Academy of Country Music Awards: Single of the Year, Video of the Year, Vocal Event of the Year, and Song of the Year, which goes to the songwriter.

When the winners were announced, Tim and Faith made four trips to the stage together—a clean sweep. Faith was five and a half months pregnant with daughter number two, Maggie Elizabeth, and Tim was glowing, too. "Just look at her," he said with admiration backstage. The Academy might just as well have elected them Nashville's First Couple, right then and there.

Music City has a unique and rich history of great male-female duos:

Conway Twitty and Loretta Lynn

Their offstage relationship was platonic, but onstage and in the studio no duet cooked hotter. Beginning with "After the Fire Is Gone" in 1971, they had no fewer than a dozen top-ten hits as a duo in a ten-year period. They were voted Vocal Duo of the Year four years running (1972–1975) by the Country Music Association.

Johnny Cash and June Carter Cash

Johnny was in the midst of a four-year drought without a number one single when he scored with "Ring of Fire" in 1963. One of the song's cowriters, June Carter, became his wife in 1968 after he proposed to her onstage during a concert. The hits they performed together include "Jackson" and "If I Were a Carpenter." Johnny and June were the CMA's Vocal Group of the Year in 1969.

George Jones and Tammy Wynette

They may have been star-crossed, but that doesn't mean George and Tammy weren't the king and queen of country music in their time. Prior to and after their mid-1970s divorce, this tandem performed sold-out concerts and recorded several solid hits together, including the number ones "We're Gonna Hold On" and "Near You."

Porter Wagoner and Dolly Parton

The CMA's Vocal Group of the Year in 1968, and Vocal Duo of the Year in 1970 and 1971, Porter and Dolly joined forces when the then unknown Dolly appeared on Porter's TV variety show. The relationship was never more than professional, and at times it was less than harmonious, but the top-five singles included classics such as "If Teardrops Were Pennies" and "Making Plans."

Kenny Rogers and Dottie West

They didn't hook up until the latter half of Dottie's career, but the union was a special one while it lasted. Legend has it that while Dottie was recording "Every Time Two Fools Collide," Kenny unexpectedly entered the studio and started to sing along. The song shot to the top of the charts in 1978. Their two other number one hits were "All I Ever Need Is You," and "What Are We Doin' in Love," and they chalked up several songs that reached the top twenty. Dottie and Kenny were the CMA's Vocal Duo of the Year in 1978 and 1979.

David Frizzell and Shelly West

The younger brother of Lefty Frizzell and the daughter of Dottie West teamed up in the early 1980s on "You're the Reason God Made

Oklahoma," which went to the top of the charts. They followed that with four other top-twenty singles, then split shortly after Shelly divorced David's little brother Allen, then reunited in 1984. David and Shelly were CMA Vocal Duo of the Year in 1981 and 1982.

Country songs have long focused on the trials and tribulations of man-woman relationships, and there are few treats fans enjoy more than the chemistry of a great guy-gal duo. There's no point in trumping up specious comparisons between Nashville's classic couples, but it can be noted that the McGraw-Hill union is the lone one among the greats in which two established solo stars work together while being married to each other without the specter of divorce on the horizon. Cash and Carter come close, but June didn't reach Faith's level of solo success. George and Tammy fit the star bill but didn't keep their marriage together.

In recent times there has been a spate of exciting one-off pairings: Shania Twain and Bryan White on "From This Moment On," Sheryl Crow and Dwight Yoakam on "Baby Don't Go," Steve Wariner and Anita Cochran on "What If I Said," Mark Chesnutt and Lee

Ann Womack on "Make Memories with Me," and Garth Brooks and Trisha Yearwood on "In Another's Eyes" to name a few. But, as fun and rewarding as those combos have been, none of them is an ongoing partnership or involves an intimate offstage relationship. And although Faith and Tim aren't a formal musical duo either, it's a good bet they'll be doing more projects together in the future, and an even safer bet that they truly mean it when they sing to each other about being in love.

"We would like to sing a song together every now and then," Tim confirms, "but as far as our careers becoming combined, I don't see that happening." Tim also asserts that he and Faith are "very different in a lot of ways . . . two very independent people." Tim and Faith both understand what it takes to make it in the music business, so they give each other the leeway to do what needs to be done. When one of them wins an award, you can see in the face of the other the pride and respect they have for the other's career accomplishments.

Yet, it's definitely family first in both their hearts, which means looking after each other's needs and those of their adorable daughters.

Tim and Faith's priorities adjusted dramatically when Gracie came into the picture. Faith took the better part of an entire year off, and Tim put limits on his workload for the first time in a long time, giving himself more time to spend at home with his wife and first daughter. Tim says his favorite pastime is simply watching Faith and Gracie sleeping on the couch, and he often sings his daughter to sleep with the old Jerry Jeff Walker (the guy who wrote "Mr. Bojangles") tune "Precious Thing." Tim has explained, "I sang that song to her from the time we knew we were having a baby. I'd use Faith's belly button like a microphone."

Her entire adult life Faith had contended that she would someday have children, and that her career would take a backseat if need be. "If I had to leave the road for my family because my kids weren't dealing with me being gone or whatever," she told *Country Weekly* in 1996, "I would just have to do that [put her career on hold]." For his part, Tim made the full transition from music man to family man, from superstar to breadwinner. He was no longer the boy who only wanted "beautiful women and throwing your sweat around." He was a man with responsibilities and commitments.

"You just have to keep in perspective that it's what you do for a living, rather than thinking it's all just about you."

—TIM

In the wake of Gracie's birth Tim and Faith grew more protective of their private lives, such as making efforts to keep Gracie's baby photos out of the media. Not that they didn't love showing her off to people, but they did want to spare her from being in the proverbial spotlight. The one well-publicized and hilarious exception was when Faith showed a photo of Gracie's bare bottom on national TV. "That's what Tim's looks like," she told the audience.

One lesson marriage often has to teach us is that the love we thought couldn't grow any deeper—the bond we thought was as strong as it would ever be—does indeed become deeper and stronger when children come along. "Faith and I have really gotten closer since Gracie Katherine was born," Tim told *Country Weekly*.

As they'd done the year before, Tim and Faith sang in the new year at the Nashville Arena. It was a star-packed affair, with Jeff Foxworthy, Martina McBride, Tanya Tucker, Johnny Paycheck, and Kenny Chesney all in attendance. It was a perfect way to storm into 1998, a year that would prove eventful for Tim and Faith.

"I just can't imagine how I can be so lucky."

—TIM

CHAPTER EIGHT

Bring the Family

Tim was back into the swing of touring, and Faith was taking care of Gracie while also making preparations for an upcoming album. They did spend Valentine's Day 1998 together in Halifax, Nova Scotia, where Tim had a show. Faith joined him onstage for "It's Your Love." It was going through the grapevine that another McGraw-Hill duet was in the works and would turn up on Faith's new release. A few folks on Music Row speculated that it would be Tim and Faith's sublime version of "When I Need You," the Leo Sayer pop classic they sometimes sing together in concert.

A lot of longtime Faith Hill fans swore that she was singing better than ever since the birth of her daughter, an observation Faith says is absolutely accurate. Some speculated it was due to changes that came in the wake of her throat operation, perhaps a strengthening from vocal exercises. Others thought it might be a simple matter of maturation, or possibly just better studio production. Faith insists hormones are the explanation. While recording *Faith* she called her friend Amy Grant and lamented that her voice wasn't responding like she had come to expect. Amy told Faith to relax and let the hormones run their course, that it all would be fine, and she was right. Faith talked about her voice with Anika Van Wyk of the *Calgary Sun*, saying, "Well, maybe it's a little stronger from singing all these years and taking time off, having Gracie and just maturing and feeling more confident."

This was without doubt the most difficult of Faith's three albums, and she has described the process as "hell" on several occasions. As she told Michael Bane, "The process was about discovering new places in myself, and that is hard, hard work." She stretches to the

> "You know, I went through Egypt to get to Cheyenne, but I finally got there."
>
> —FAITH

stylistic outer edges and pushes her vocal range to the limit throughout *Faith*, and her sheer ambition is inspiring in itself. This is not an artist who sits still and hopes her audience will, too. "I could not have gone deeper to find what this record is," Faith asserts.

One critic noted that Faith had "never sounded more passionate or sophisticated," and another enthused that "she demonstrates here that a little infusion of rhythm doesn't diminish the considerable warmth and appeal of her singing." True, every musician believes and/or claims their newest work is not only their best but also a departure from their usual fare, but *Faith* honestly is both those things.

Faith admits that she had reached a point at which she didn't even want to listen to music. That's when she'd known it was time to take a break. But after a three-year hiatus she plunged back into the studio. As she told Janet E. Williams, "Like in a barrel of hot coals, headfirst." The fact that Faith had taken so much time off and done so much evolving between albums meant there was little chance of *Faith* sounding like any previous Faith Hill release. As she was fond of

> "I was at a great place where I felt I
> could take some time to reinvent."
> —FAITH

telling interviewers, "It went into the refrigerator hot liquid and came out a beautiful salad, full of wonderful fruit."

Among the choice pieces are "My Wild Frontier," a mournful and yet redemptive song about a woman whose husband dies shortly after the birth of their child. "Her soul mate passes away, but he leaves this child that is a part of him. Even though he is gone, there is still a bond that is stronger than anything else on earth."

One of the hookiest tunes on the album is "The Secret of Life," a Gretchen Peters song whose verse structure is rather reminiscent of Sheryl Crow's "All I Want to Do." Interestingly, the album's closing track, "Somebody Stand by Me," was cowritten by Sheryl Crow. "I'm a fan of Crow's and I just love that song," Faith told Jim Caligiuri. Crow—a former backup singer for rock and pop legends Rod Stewart, Eric Clapton, Don Henley, and Michael Jackson—made fans of numerous country artists with her solo albums. Trisha Yearwood reviewed Crow's self-titled second album in *New Country*, saying "I think Sheryl has a connection to country music. . . . If I was making rock 'n' roll records, I'd want to make that kind of record."

From the underrated Matraca Berg (who cowrote "Strawberry Wine," the CMA's 1997 Song of the Year, performed by Deana Carter) to the legendary Diane Warren (writer of the Trisha Yearwood/LeAnn Rimes smash "How Do I Live"), *Faith* is stuffed to the gills with fine songwriters. There are even songs by eighties rockers Aldo Nova and Billy Burnette (who stepped in on guitar when Lindsey Buckingham left Fleetwood Mac).

The album is also brimming with top guest vocal talent, including Vince Gill, whose distinctive and subtle backup vocals grace "Let Me Let Go." "From the moment he opened his mouth," Faith says of Vince's performance, "we knew it was more than just harmony." Vince isn't the only famous country crooner to turn up on *Faith*; a fellow by the name of Tim McGraw chimes in on "Just to Hear You Say You Love Me."

Of course the jewel of the album is the crossover hit "This Kiss," which topped the country charts and reached the upper echelons of the pop charts. Faith soars and swoops to the heavens with a joyful performance, and the song is irresistible. Beth Nielsen Chapman not only cowrote the song, she also backs Faith's vocals to perfection. Faith explains,

"Because she cowrote 'This Kiss,' we invited her to sing on it and she ended up creating a completely new harmony section. . . . We already had a great song, but Beth was capable of taking it even further."

The album is unique from a production standpoint, in that five of the twelve songs were produced by Faith and Dann Huff, while the remaining seven were produced by Faith and Byron Gallimore. Dann and Byron did their work separate from each other, with Faith as the common link. Between them Dann and Byron recorded a whopping twenty-eight songs, with a quarter of them making the final cut.

Faith had never worked with either Byron or Dann, as ex-fiance Scott Hendricks had produced her two previous albums. Byron is, of course, one of Tim's coproducers, so Faith was familiar with his work. She contacted Dann on the recommendation of Mutt Lange, who is Shania Twain's husband and one of the world's most respected producers and a terrific judge of talent.

On March 14, 1998, in Phoenix, Faith and Tim joined the eighteen-show George Strait tour that would run through June. For a mere

$25, fans could catch a truckload of the hottest acts in country music including Faith and Tim, and, of course, The Man himself, George Strait. "This is the biggest tour that country's ever had. It's just a whole different deal. And it's very cool," Tim crowed.

The group tour has become all the rage, but this was the first time country had ever gone this large. Tim seemed actually to prefer the big stadiums in some respects. "You don't feel as threatened, like when it's 200 or 300 people just staring right at you," he told Brian McCollum in the *Detroit Free Press*. His goal was to hit the stage running and enjoy himself to the max. "We try to have fun up onstage. When you're entertaining each other, you're going to please the crowd," he asserts.

With both her parents on tour, Gracie got her first taste of traveling. She slept all through her first night on the bus, but not so the second. "She was up all night. I think she was a little scared," Tim explained. But it didn't take long for Gracie to adjust, and she was soon back to her outgoing self. Learning to travel is part of being a member of the McGraw-Hill clan, and there's no doubt that the children will develop into "citizens of the

"We've covered all of the outlets and tried to baby-proof it as much as possible, as fast as she's growing— and she is WILD! A wild child."

—FAITH

world." A nanny is available when Faith is doing a show or an interview, but the rest of the time the kids are with one or both of their folks.

Tim and Faith have logged countless hours on buses, which Faith, for one, prefers over planes. It goes without saying that they also love to take vacations, especially to the beaches of the Caribbean and Hawaii. "Anywhere the sun is hot, we have fun," is how Tim puts it. Camping in Montana—the state where they became engaged—is another favorite. Most country stars love to visit and perform in New York City, and Tim and Faith are no exceptions. Faith has commented, "New York audiences are wonderful. They're fun, excitable, and they really listen to the music. . . . Plus there's all this great shopping and food."

Of course, their life isn't all exotic locales and cross-country tours; in fact, Tim and Faith are most happy at their home—a lovely and modest four-bedroom colonial in Brentwood, Tennessee—cooking Italian food, watching TV, riding horses (some of which are Mr. Jeff, Lacy Daisy, Dizzie Rose, Image, Joker, and Ms. Audrey), and walking with their dogs (Whitley, Dakota, Roaddog, Grant). The one constant in the McGraw-Hill household is laughter—

this is one of the happiest homes you could ever hope to see.

When her hubbie is watching the kids, Faith likes to write letters or read her mail. She loves to rent old movies and flip through her photo albums. She'll spend an afternoon riding four-wheelers, playing tennis, or she'll "just piddle around the house." She has a large collection of old picture frames. Tim puts in hours working on his farm, which he doesn't have time to manage on a full-time basis but which is still one of his favorite places to be. He's stockpiled a collection of motorcycles that he rides when time allows. He also plays golf. Tim and Faith both like to water ski and play softball.

In mid-April Faith performed live for CMT viewers from a seventy-year-old brick factory located near Franklin, Tennessee. The stage was artfully designed to resemble a New York City loft, with hand-woven rugs, candles, and a big overstuffed sofa and chair. Faith, who was five months pregnant with her second child, got help from Vince Gill on "Let Me Let Go," and Tim joined her for "When I Need You," the Leo Sayer song that has become one

"This is the most rewarding thing that's ever happened to me in my life."
—TIM on his wife and children

"Oh, I love changing diapers—and I'm good at it."
—TIM

of Faith and Tim's hallmark duets, at least onstage.

Faith and Tim were out on tour through the summer, playing at state fairs and music festivals—the standard country circuit and still the best method for getting in touch with the fans. Looking to take his live shows to even higher excitement levels in terms of production, in September Tim got new lights, new sound, and a new stage design. "We don't want to get away from what we've been doing, but it's all pretty exciting," he enthused. Fans who have followed his career say Tim is getting better and better in concert, and that's saying something since he has always shined onstage.

Faith worked to support her new album, right up to the point when it was time for her second child to arrive. "Faith had to have been a marine in a former life," Tim joked in *Country Weekly*. She noted that the new baby was "carrying differently" than Gracie had; in other words, the new baby didn't seem to be in position precisely the same. Morning sickness wasn't a significant problem, nor were her food cravings as strong as they were during her first pregnancy. Tim and Faith chose not to learn the sex of the child in advance of the birth, opting instead to enjoy the surprise. As for Gracie, she was aware that her mommy's tummy was getting bigger and bigger, and she learned to say the word "baby," but otherwise she was too young to grasp the ramifications of what was soon going to happen: that a sibling was on the way. A week after Tim and Faith received their eight 1998 CMA Award nominations, Maggie Elizabeth McGraw was born.

It goes without mentioning that the future is wide open and bright for Tim, Faith, Gracie, and Maggie. There'll no doubt be more little ones to come, since both Tim and Faith speak often of having a big family. More hit duets are surely in the works, too. In fact, Tim told Rex Rutkowski in *Modern Screen's Country Music* that they "would love to do an album together someday." He also perfectly summed up what'll make that album one of the most anticipated of the year, and what makes everything Faith and Tim do together worthy of anticipation: "We complete each other in every way."

Don't miss a single one of these outstanding biographies.

Published by Ballantine Books.
Available in your local bookstore.